AF328577

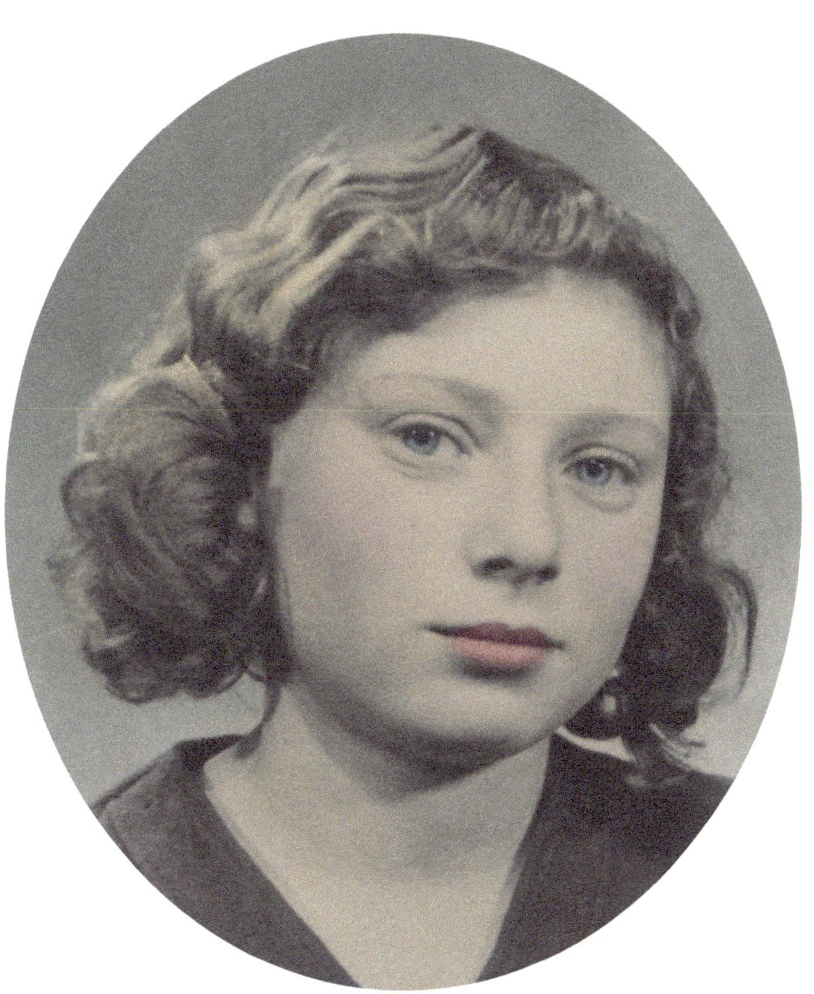

First published in 2019
by Real Film and Publishing
www.realfp.com.au

Cataloguing-in-Publication data is available from the
National Library of Australia

When The Walls Have Ears

ISBN 978-0-6484056-2-7

Written by Ruth Hampel and Romy Moshinsky
Edited by Georgie Raik-Allen
Editorial assistance by Abigail Hough
Design by Trisha Garner

A MEMOIR

WHEN THE WALLS HAVE EARS

RUTH HAMPEL

CONTENTS

PROLOGUE

Like many idealistic young communists, my parents worshipped
Joseph Stalin and passionately believed the Marxist promise
of 'a workers' paradise'. In 1930, we moved from Chemnitz
to Leningrad to pursue their communist dream. Despite their
unwavering devotion, during the Great Purge my parents were falsely
denounced as traitors and Stalin's henchmen stormed our home one
night to take away my father. We never heard from him again. Half a
century later I discovered that my father had been executed 19 days
after his arrest.

My mother was also arrested and accused of treason. She was
thrown into jail, forced to sign a false confession and sentenced
to hard labour at a collective farm in Kazakhstan. As a young girl
of seven, I was branded the daughter of traitors and continuously
hounded by the secret police.

Years later I was reunited with my mother in Kazakhstan.
By then she was a broken woman: paralysed by fear, paranoia
and the pain of not knowing what had happened to her husband.
Together, we somehow managed to survive the war and the perilous
journey towards a new home.

It was only 10 years ago, when I read *The Whisperers*[1] –
"an encyclopaedia of woe"[2] – about the trauma that affected
ordinary Russian families and citizens during the violent and
repressive reign of Stalin that I began to fully comprehend what
my mother and I had lived through. Reading the unearthed diaries
and testimonies of survivors of Stalin's tyranny opened the scars
from my childhood wounds. I discovered that I was a member
of 'Stalin's lost generation' and began my journey towards better
understanding my mentally fragile mother and forgiving myself
for my own shortcomings as a daughter. Writing this book has also
been an integral part of my healing.

------

1 *The Whisperers – Private Life in Stalin's Russia* by Orlando Figes, 2007.
2 *The Economist*, Arts Review, 18 October 2007.

PART ONE

EUROPE AND SOVIET CENTRAL ASIA

1930—1949

*(Previous page) My father's grandparents
with my father's cousin in Poland c.1904
(This page) My father at 14, c.1918*

GREAT EXPECTATIONS

My paternal grandparents, Leibl and Chana Fuks, lived in Chemnitz, Germany near the border of Czechoslovakia and Poland. Every time my grandmother was pregnant, she would travel back to her parents' home in the Polish town of Brzeziny, 20 kilometres east of Lodz, to give birth. My aunt Rosa was born in Brzeziny in 1902 and two years later, on 20 February 1904, my father Max was born. They had two younger siblings, Bertha[1] and Sam.[2]

Chemnitz was a large industrial town in the northern foothills of the Ore Mountains. My grandfather and his brothers owned a textile factory specialising in knitwear that was successful enough to warrant a chauffeur-driven company car. When the car was unavailable, my father's family would make use of the modern electric trams that had recently been installed in the town. My father grew up in a comfortable home and had a good education. After finishing school, he moved to nearby Dresden to attend university where he studied electrical engineering.

1 Born 1906

2 Born 1910

My father dressed up for Purim

(Clockwise from above left) My paternal great grandmother, my paternal grandmother in 1938, my maternal grandfather and father in Paris, 1926

*(Left) My paternal grandfather
and aunt Bertha's children
(Right) My aunt Rosa and paternal grandfather*

My mother, Stella, was also the second-born in a family of four
children. She had an older brother named Max, a younger brother
named Marek and a younger sister named Eugenia (Jenny). My
maternal grandmother, Carola (Caroline), would also travel from
Germany to her parents' home in Warsaw for the births of her
children. My mother was born on 26 February 1904 and, a few
weeks later, was bundled up and returned to the family home
in Chemnitz. Jenny was the only one in the family to be born
in Germany because the outbreak of World War I prevented my
grandmother from travelling to Poland.

My maternal grandfather, Morrice Muszkatblat, was a sales
representative with a paper company, where he earned enough for
the family to live in a spacious apartment. My grandparents valued
education and all four of their children were encouraged to finish
high school and, where possible, attend university. My mother
excelled at languages and spoke French, Russian and German
fluently. She also spoke a little English. After school she completed
a secretarial course.

There was a synagogue in Chemnitz but no Jewish schools
so most Jewish learning took place in the home. But my mother's
family was far more interested in communism than religion.
Post-war Germany was politically and economically unstable and
the family had become increasingly drawn to Marxist ideology;
collectively they longed to play a role in the establishment
of the promised 'workers' paradise'. To fulfil this dream, my
grandmother's sister Helena and her husband Branek moved to
Leningrad in Russia while my mother was still a child. Tragically,
several years later, the couple were somehow caught up in the
Russian Revolution and were killed on a train trying to return to

My mother during her teenage years

At nine months

Germany. My mother's family was known in Chemnitz as the 'pink' or 'red ones'. This was compounded when my grandmother's three brothers, Edward, Heinrich and Florian, all moved to Moscow with their widowed mother Eva (my great-grandmother) in the 1920s. Eva died in 1930 so I never had the chance to meet her.

I do not know how my parents met, but presumably they moved in the same social circle and attended the same dances hosted for the youth of the town. My father was a fun-loving prankster and my mother was drawn to his sense of humour and intelligence. They were a very good-looking couple, they were devoted to each other and they shared a love of communism. Their common desire to live in Russia strengthened their bond. My parents became engaged in 1924 but delayed their wedding because my father was still studying for his degree. They eventually married in 1927.

Not long afterwards, the ties between the Fuks and Muszkatblat families were reinforced when my father's sister Rosa married my mother's brother Max. They soon had a baby daughter named Sonia and began planning their move to Moscow.

The early years of my parents' marriage were relatively carefree. They holidayed at the Fuks family's summerhouse in Brzeziny in Poland and socialised with their many friends and large extended family. In 1929, they were thrilled to discover that my mother was expecting, and, after a healthy pregnancy, they welcomed me into the world on 9 January 1930.

My father the prankster (centre),
uncle Marek (middle right)
and mother (front right)

*My father's family with my father
and pregnant mother (front), 1929*

My father in his student days at Dresden University

(Above centre) My father in the snow
showing that he is penniless

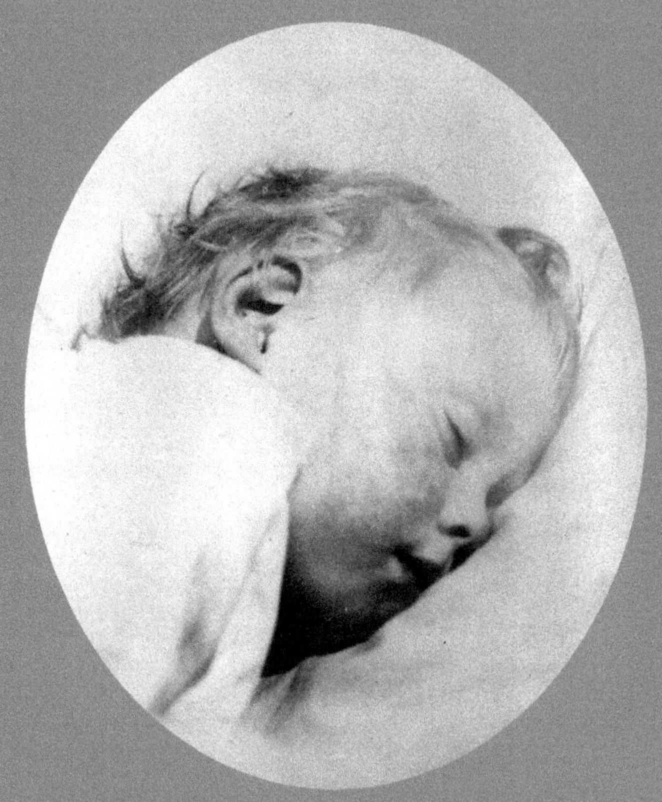

At one year

COMMUNIST DREAMING

In November 1930, when I was 10 months old, my parents fulfilled their communist dream when we moved to Leningrad.[1] My earliest memory of Leningrad is from soon after we first arrived. The apartment we had been allocated was not ready, so we were accommodated in a dwelling outside the city, somewhere near the station. I remember my father pushing me in my pink pram along the railway line one sunny day. That happy memory, of a simple time with my loving father, remains clear in my mind, even though I was only a baby at the time.[2]

As Hitler's power grew, life for our remaining family in Germany was becoming increasingly difficult. My father's parents made the bold decision to sell their textile business and move back to Poland. Meanwhile, my mother's parents and siblings submitted their passports to the embassy in Berlin to obtain visas that would allow them to join us in the Soviet Union. Before the visas were issued, in 1933, a law was passed revoking German

---

1 Leningrad was renamed St Petersburg in 1991 after the collapse of the Soviet Union.

2 Many decades later I asked my mother if that early memory could possibly be correct and she confirmed that it was true; my father had loved taking me for walks in my pram along the railway line.

citizenship from Eastern European Jews and my grandfather
Morrice, a Polish citizen, was given 48 hours' notice to leave the
country. The authorities also ordered my mother's brother Marek
to exit Germany because of his communist leanings, so Morrice
and Marek fled to Paris together. It was decided that my aunt Jenny
would join them as soon as she reclaimed their passports from
the embassy. On three occasions, Jenny travelled to the embassy
in Berlin and returned empty-handed. Finally the embassy clerk
admitted that the documents were lost. Furious, Jenny abused
the German clerk, telling him to shove the papers up his behind!
Luckily, she was not arrested for such insolence. Without any doc-
umentation, Jenny travelled to Paris to join her father and brother.

My grandmother stayed behind in Chemnitz to liquidate their
remaining assets and pack up their belongings. My mother and
I returned to Germany to say goodbye to my grandmother before
her departure. It was considered too dangerous for my father to
travel with us, as he had already applied for Russian citizenship
and the German authorities may have been tempted to detain
him. I remember the emptiness of my grandparents' apartment –
everything had been sent to Paris, except for a huge chest that sat
in the middle of the lounge room. I vividly remember being given
coloured buttons to play with while my mother and grandmother
spoke to each other in hushed tones.

On the way back to Leningrad, my mother and I stayed
overnight with friends in Berlin. I do not know if the family was
Jewish or if they were non-Jewish friends that my parents had met
through their communist networks. I remember my mother holding
me in her arms that night as we peered out of their darkened
third-floor apartment to the street below where we could see Nazis

*(Above) This is the only photo I have of myself
with both my parents, Leningrad, 1931*

(Above) My maternal grandparents
with Jenny in Paris, 1933
(Below) My uncle Marek

marching with their torches. As a three-year-old, I was entranced by the flames but also conscious of the palpable fear in the room. In later life, I realised that the parade was a celebration of the appointment of Hitler as chancellor of Germany. It was 30 January 1933.

In Paris, my uncle Marek was fortunate to be able to resume his university studies in medicine. My grandfather found work as a paper salesman; he did not speak French and his writing skills were poor but he managed to earn a meagre living, partly because he was such a gentle and personable man. My aunt supplemented the family income by hairdressing. The family lived together in a small apartment with a communal bathroom in the 9th *arrondissement*. Adjusting to their new life in Paris was a struggle, but the family was grateful to be out of Hitler's reach and made the best of their situation. At university, Marek soon met a young Polish woman named Eva who was also studying to be a doctor, and who he would later marry. Around the same time, Jenny met her future husband, Nathan.

Back in the Soviet Union, there was no such thing as unemployment for hard-working, idealistic people like my parents. Vladimir Lenin's slogan, 'He who does not work shall not eat'[3] was a key principle in the preliminary phase of the evolution towards a communist society. My parents were given employment, accommodation and other privileges to help them become accustomed to the climate and conditions. It was part of the indoctrination process but, in reality, my parents had been brainwashed before they arrived.

My mother went to an office each day where she worked translating French and German into Russian. My father worked in a huge factory that produced armaments, possibly airplanes. It was later rumoured that the factory was secretly

---

3 This phrase, taken from the New Testament, appears in Lenin's 1917 work, *The State and Revolution*.

making weapons for the Germans. I was once told that 9000 people worked at the factory.[4]

In Leningrad we were allocated a four-bedroom apartment in a building designated for foreigners.[5] There was nothing else in the street at the time except our apartment building, which was part of a private estate formerly owned by a duke. The duke did not have children, so he donated the estate in 1908 to an organisation that housed unmarried mothers and their children – hence our street was known as 'Children's Street'. I cannot recall how many apartments were in the building but we were surrounded by young communists from England, France and Germany.

Our apartment was fully furnished but we had also brought every imaginable household item with us from Germany. The female Russian caretaker greeted us by saying, "Tell me, is this how the unemployed in Germany live?" My parents were pleased that we had cold running water, which was a rarity at the time in Leningrad. The apartment had three large rooms including a big lounge and dining room, and a kitchen. I remember we had a red table with drawers that were used as sinks. There was a communal bath and toilet in the hallway.

My early childhood in Leningrad was a happy time and I wanted for nothing. I adored my fun-loving father – my mother was the more serious of the two – and was always referred to as 'Max's daughter'. My first nanny was called Erna. She was a 'Volga German' who claimed to be a direct descendant of German farmers brought to Russia in the late 18th century by Catherine the Great to modernise the country's agriculture industry. Erna lived with us

---

4 I have also heard that up to 90,000 people were employed at the factory, which seems absurd.

5 I have been back to that apartment building twice. The first time, in the 1990s after Gorbachev came to power, the building was being used as an army barracks and it looked dilapidated and filthy. My guide asked for permission to enter but I stood at the door and did not have the courage to go in. I went back a second time with my children in 2010. When my grandson returned a few years later, the house had been turned into a school.

My father at work in Leningrad, 1936

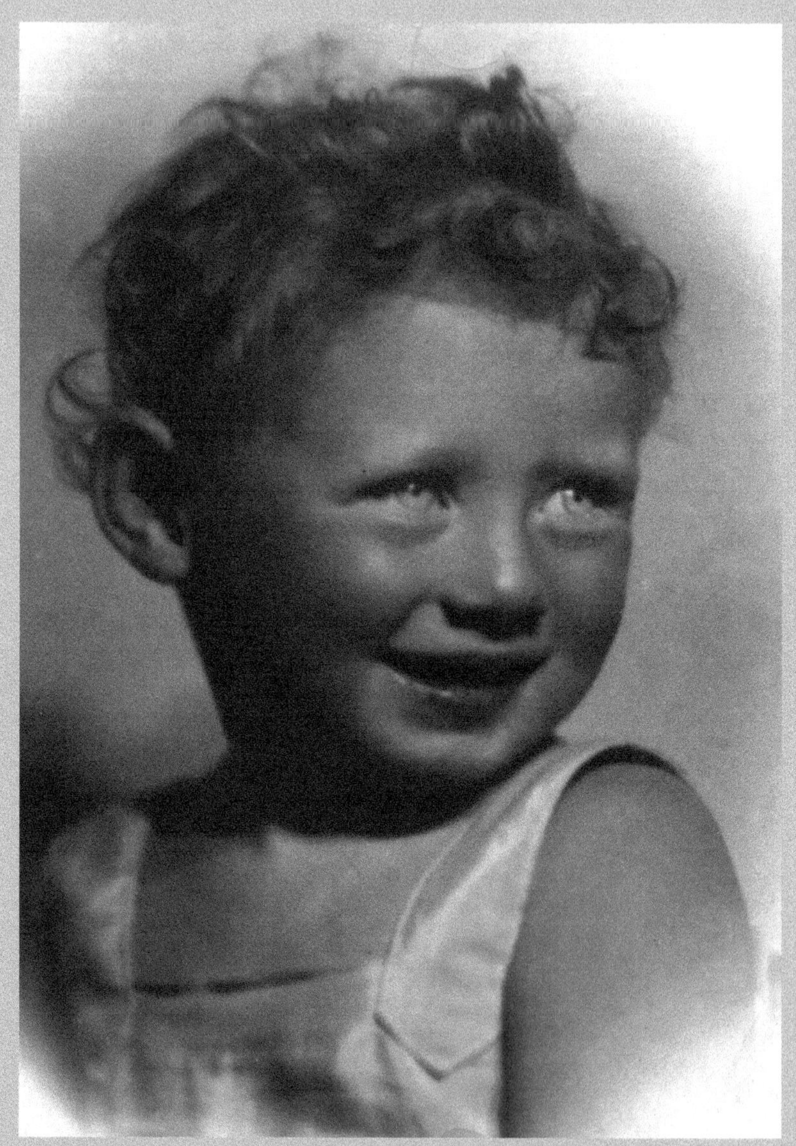

Age four

until I was four years old and I remember loving her dearly. I was upset when she left but she continued to visit our family regularly. After Erna, I had a Russian nanny whose name I cannot remember. I must have been a skinny child as she would make kasha[6] with milk and butter to fatten me up. The oily skin would float on the top and I refused to eat it. To this day, I cannot eat porridge. She then tried to feed me in our building's communal canteen[7], believing that I would be more inclined to finish my meals if there were other people around.

From an early age I spent a lot of time with my much-loved great-aunt Musa. She was a Russian woman who was married to one of my mother's cousins, Edward Muszkatblat. Edward had a daughter named Stella from a previous marriage[8] but Musa had no children of her own and she showered me with love and attention. Before the revolution, Musa had been a wealthy woman with a six-storey house. After the revolution, Musa was fortunate to be able to retain the top floor of the house, which had been the ballroom. She turned the ballroom into an apartment that retained its former glory and was covered in the colourful silk flowers Musa made as a living.

I have fond memories of going on holiday with Musa when I was four years old. We visited her cousins who had a small farm outside Leningrad. One of the little piglets on the farm took a liking to me and followed me everywhere. I also have a vivid memory of holidaying with my parents in a resort outside Leningrad designated for high-ranking communists. One night, I was allowed to stay awake to see a fire-eater perform. Every night I would beg my parents to let me stay awake until the sun went

---

6 Kasha is a traditional type of Russian porridge made from buckwheat.

7 The canteen, which was open for breakfast and lunch, was originally the kitchen in the duke's house.

8 Stella was given the unfortunate nickname of 'the ugly Stella' in our family because my mother was always referred to as 'the beautiful Stella'.

down at 10.30pm. Most often I holidayed with my uncle Max, aunt Rosa and cousin Sonia in a summerhouse near Moscow while my parents enjoyed a peaceful holiday without me in Crimea.

In Leningrad, we had privileged access to the 'closed shop' for foreigners where we were able to buy anything we wanted. On his day off, my father would walk me to the shop and buy me an orange and a chocolate. There was an unspoken agreement that I would not tell my mother about the chocolate. Other times we shopped at the nearby bazaar, a farmers' market where peasants would bring fresh produce to sell twice a week. I would go there regularly with my mother. These special benefits made us wilfully blind to the reality of Stalin's dictatorship; his draconian policies had resulted in a famine that, from 1932 to 1933, killed millions of people in the grain-producing regions of the Soviet Union, particularly in the Ukraine, which had formerly been known as the breadbasket of Europe.

At first, I attended a German-speaking kindergarten. When I turned six, I moved to a Russian-speaking kindergarten near my father's work. For me it was a carefree time, except for the many illnesses I contracted. It was before the widespread availability of vaccinations and I contracted measles, German measles, chicken pox and diphtheria. The illnesses had to be endured without access to any medication. My mother would call on a Russian lady in the building to treat me with cupping therapy – the darker the circles left on my small body, the more successful she considered the treatment.

My father was granted Russian citizenship in 1936. Before he became a citizen, the government had been generous, but afterwards we were no different to other suffering Russians.

My father became a citizen at lunchtime and, by the time he arrived home, the authorities had removed our access to the kitchen in the apartment. My mother had to plead for a small stove, a saucepan, some cutlery and crockery.

—————————

(Above) With Sonia and a friend in a spa town near Leningrad, 1934 (Below) Celebrating New Year's Eve in Leningrad, 1934. It was forbidden to celebrate Christmas but, for the first time, we were allowed a 'New Year tree'

*My mother's cousin Stella with
Uncle Sam in Leningrad, 1937*

A KNOCK ON THE DOOR

fondly remember my close friend, Sonia Zoebel, who lived in our building. Like me, Sonia was an only child, she was the same age, and her family was also from Germany. I do not think they were Jewish, but that was never relevant.

Sonia's father was the first person I saw being taken away. It was the summer of 1936 on a 'free day' (in the Soviet Union, the week was only six days long and the sixth day was a rest day). I was playing outside when I saw two members of the secret police arrest Sonia's father in broad daylight with his hands cuffed behind his back. It was devastating because he worked at the same factory as my father and we knew him very well.

Before that arrest, I had been unaware of the purges that were terrorising the country. The Great Purge, or Great Terror as it later became known, was Stalin's campaign of political repression designed to eliminate challenges from opposition groups. It involved widespread police surveillance, suspicion, oppression, imprisonments and arbitrary executions based on trumped-up claims of espionage.[1]

---

1 It is estimated that 600,000 people died at the hands of the Stalin-led Soviet government during the purges from 1936–1938.

The Soviet 'principle of collective responsibility' determined that one was responsible for the actions of others in the family. We had no idea what Sonia's father had allegedly done – we just knew him to be a lovely man – but he was now considered a traitor, an enemy of the people, and everyone began to avoid the family for fear of being found guilty by association. Even as a child I understood what was meant by the expression 'the walls have ears'. There could have been a spy living in our building but, despite the paranoia and genuine fear, my mother took me by the hand and we went to Sonia's apartment to visit the grieving family. I remember seeing Sonia's mother sitting at the table crying. She looked stunned.

Throughout that summer, others from our building began to disappear during the night. My mother was petrified that my father would also be taken by the secret police, but he refused to believe it was possible because he had not done anything wrong. He would repeat that it could not happen to him, because he had not committed any crime. To the contrary, he remained devoted to the party and to his work.

In August 1937, my father had his appendix removed. I remember going to the hospital and crying hysterically when I was told that children were not allowed to visit. Finally a nurse relented and allowed me to see him, as long as I wore a white doctor's coat tied up with a belt. It was a particularly tense time in our household, exacerbated by the arrival of my father's mother who came from Poland to stay with us while my father recuperated. Earlier, my father's younger brother, Sam, had also come to live with us after finishing university in Germany. I vaguely remember that he had his own room and kitchenette in our building.

One day, a neighbour from upstairs came to our apartment and told my parents he was returning to Germany. My father said, "Are you crazy?" He said, "No. It can't be any worse than it is here". Then he said a crude expression, *"Wenn sie dich brauchen, stopfen sie dir Honig in den Arsch, aber wenn sie dich nicht brauchen, machen sie dich einen Kopf kürzer"*, meaning, "When they need you, they stuff honey in your ass, but if they don't need you, they make you a head shorter". He left Russia soon after.

During this period, my mother asked my father to convince his mother to go to Moscow to stay with my aunty Rosa and uncle Max. My mother thought Moscow might be safer and, possibly, she needed a break from her mother-in-law. My grandmother left at the end of August.

I started school on 1 September 1937. Two days later, on 3 September, my father was taken away. Until the secret police came to our door in the middle of the night, my father had refused to admit he might be under suspicion. Nevertheless, when my father heard the bootsteps approaching our apartment he woke my mother and told her, "They are here for me". Then there was a knock on the door.

When I got up early the next morning, I found my mother crying on the divan. She told me that the secret police had taken my father away. But she insisted that I still go to school saying, "You must put on a brave face and not tell anybody what has happened". That morning, she did not tell me that the secret police had also produced a warrant to arrest her, my uncle Sam and my grandmother (who had just left) on 30 September. The warrant gave us less than a month's notice to prepare for the arrests. What could be done? Special papers were needed to travel anywhere and, by then, it was too late to leave.

In the years that followed his arrest, we had no idea if my father was alive or dead. We were left with only our memories to sustain us, and the gigantic void left in his wake. Many decades later, in October 2001, it was confirmed that my beloved father was executed on 20 September 1937 – 17 days after his arrest. We do not know what crime he was accused of but, presumably, he refused to sign any admission of guilt, so he was ordered to die. My father's death certificate states that he was executed in Leningrad. It came as a shock to me that he was imprisoned and killed in the same city where we had lived together, and it continues to pain me that, in the terrifying weeks after his disappearance, he had been close to us but beyond our grasp.

Stalin – our hero, our father, our god – was in fact just a tyrant who did whatever he liked, including ordering the summary execution of innocent people. I always question, who learned from whom? Hitler from Stalin, or Stalin from Hitler?

Somehow, my uncle Sam managed to take me to my relatives in Moscow on 30 September. How he accomplished this when there was a warrant for his arrest and he had no money, I will never know. I have no memory of saying goodbye to my mother, so it is possible she was taken during the night before we boarded the train.

On the night they arrested my father, the secret police locked our wardrobes but my mother had pleaded with the agents to leave out some of my clothes, which she packed into a small suitcase. After the 10-hour train journey to Moscow, Sam left me holding my suitcase on the doorstep of my aunt and uncle's home. Fearing that his presence would endanger his mother, his sister Rosa and his brother-in-law Max, he quickly gave me a kiss and returned to the station. We later learned that when he got off the train in Leningrad, he was immediately arrested and sent to Uzbekistan.

My mother was imprisoned for three months without charge. During that time, she hoped and prayed that my father was still alive; she was fearful for him but also for herself because the wives of executed men were usually sent away to the Gulags.[2] Finally, my mother was called in to be interrogated. It was at that point she discovered she was accused of planning to poison the water reserves in the event of war. At first, she refused to confess to any of the preposterous crimes the secret police were alleging – she knew nothing about water except how to turn on the tap! She and other inmates were then forced to stand 25 centimetres away from the wall and, if they fell asleep while standing, they were struck on the legs with chains. After five nights of this torture and no sleep, she finally agreed to sign a confession. She was given a blank piece of paper and a pencil to sign. This struck her as strange – how could she know what they would write above her signature? So she asked for a pen and she filled in the whole piece of paper with ink, except for a small box with her signature, so that nothing further could be added to the page.

Written on the walls of my mother's prison were the words:

Who wasn't, will be.
And who was, will never forget it.

My mother was not a traitor, but she had been forced to confess to conspiring against the state.

---

2 Gulags were the forced-labour camps that, from the 1920s to the mid-1950s, housed political prisoners and criminals of the Soviet Union. Millions of prisoners died in the camps due to a combination of long working hours, harsh climatic and other conditions, inadequate food, and summary executions.

My father's death certificate
issued in October 2001

With Sonia (right)

DAUGHTER OF TRAITORS

I was seven years and nine months old when I moved in with my uncle Max, aunt Rosa and 'double-cousin' Sonia. I worried that I would never see my parents or uncle again and I missed them terribly. Max was also filled with fear for his sister and Rosa fretted for her two brothers. It must have been difficult for them to console me when they were so upset themselves and worrying about the purges and their own unknowable fate.

To make matters worse, my grandmother Chana was still in Moscow when I arrived. She adored my cousin Sonia but had always treated me quite cruelly. I do not know why. Perhaps she did not like my mother and transferred her feelings onto me. I was wary of my grandmother from the previous holidays I had spent with her, Max, Rosa and Sonia at the summerhouse outside Moscow. My mother would pack me a case of clothes that she had embroidered herself (she was a wonderful seamstress) but my grandmother would not let me wear any of them because they would get dirty. She would insist that I wear the old, ill-fitting clothes that she had managed to find.

Every night after my arrival, as though to punish me, my grandmother would fill my bath with scalding hot water and force me to get in quickly. On one occasion, the water was so hot that I fainted. I still remember the feeling of becoming enveloped by darkness and trying to slide out of the bath so as not to drown. Rosa would challenge my grandmother about the temperature of the water but she would insist the bath needed to be hot enough for her to bathe afterwards. This made no sense as there was plenty of water and an automatic gas-heating system in their home, all of which was provided for free by the state.

After one month, my grandmother finally returned to Poland. Many years later, Sonia told me that she was moved to the ghetto in Lodz with her own mother and mother-in-law (aged 93 and 96) and that, one day, she was killed by a stray bullet. I do not know what happened to my two great-grandmothers but presumably they also died in the ghetto or were later sent to the gas chambers by the Nazis.

My uncle and aunt had a very good apartment with modern amenities, as well as a housekeeper whose wages were also funded by the state. Again, it was all part of the acclimatisation period during which we were being spoiled for being foreign communists. However, money was tight as Max had recently been forced to take extended leave from his job as a chemical scientist. A co-worker had warned him that someone in the company was envious and was plotting to denounce him in order to take over his position. The co-worker strongly advised my uncle to get a doctor's certificate stating that he was incapacitated and unable to work for at least a year. My uncle took heed of this advice and paid a bribe to a doctor to secure the certificate. By the time I joined the family in Moscow, Max had been out of work for 10 months. My aunt had a heart condition that caused her to regularly faint,

Aunty Rosa and Uncle Max in Moscow, 1936

(Left) Sonia and Sam, 1936
(Right) With Sonia, 1938

but she was able to work as a German tutor to help make ends
meet. In Soviet Russia, adults had to be particularly careful
about what was said in front of children, lest any indiscretions be
repeated in the outside world. So I learned all of this from being
an inquisitive child, accustomed to eavesdropping whenever
adults started whispering around me. I also remember my uncle
selling a good coat so that we would have enough money to eat.
Eventually my uncle secured a part-time job teaching chemistry
at the university.

There was no word in Russian for 'cousin' so Sonia referred to
me as her '*vtorichnyj sestra*' meaning 'secondary sister'. We shared
a birthday but she was five years older than me. We were both
only children, which was not unusual at the time but, later, the
Soviets encouraged citizens to have larger families. In the 1940s,
Stalin even introduced the honorary title of 'Mother Heroine' for
those who had more than 10 children. As only children, Sonia and
I were accustomed to a lot of attention and it was challenging for
Sonia to share her parents as well as her bedroom with me. We
loved each other but we also fought often. We were acting out –
both responding to, and adding to, the tension in the home.

At first, I was not allowed to attend school because I was
branded the daughter of traitors. That was part of the punishment
meted out by the state. So it became necessary for Max and
Rosa to formally adopt me, a process that took three months.
I remember it was a particularly confusing and lonely time. With
no friends and little to fill my day, I was in a fragile emotional
state but I still tried my best to be a model child for Max and Rosa.

After the adoption, I kept my own surname but I started
to refer to Max and Rosa as my parents and they did their best to
show me love and fully accept me into their family. My aunt was

a terrific knitter and I remember her unravelling old pullovers to knit me new jumpers; it was an expression of her love and commitment to caring for me.

Finally, I was allowed to attend school. Despite the adoption, I remained a marked child and, at times, the teachers discriminated against me. I remember the shame of being the last child in the class to be given a red handkerchief to wear around my neck, signifying acceptance into the communist youth organisation the Young Pioneers.

Sonia attended a German high school until it closed in 1938 and then she went to a Russian school. I went to School 272. The director of my primary school was a Jewish lady who taught Russian and maths. One day, presumably because of my surname, she asked me if I was Jewish. I was eight years old and I did not know what she was talking about. It was obvious to the teacher that I had absolutely no idea that I was Jewish and that seemed to trouble her. I remember her saying defiantly that we should be proud of our heritage. Later that night, I asked my uncle about being Jewish and he whispered that it was a 'religious thing' that had nothing to do with us.

I excelled at maths and I loved learning history. Of course we were only taught a version of Russian history that depicted communists as heroes; anything that did not fit into the communist doctrine was ignored or whitewashed. The only struggle I had at school was with my handwriting. I was naturally left-handed, which was deemed unacceptable in the Soviet Union – there was only the good hand and the bad hand – so I was made to write with my right hand, which I hated and my written work suffered.

A few of the children in my class lived in our compound, including a girl named Lily who lived in my building. School finished at midday and, after eating lunch, we would play together in the playground before going inside to do homework. We were also friends with a Greek girl called Helen but she was a piano prodigy, so she had to practise rather than playing with us in the sandpit or skating with us on the ice during winter.

At eight

SECRET HOPE

At the beginning of 1938, my aunty received a parcel. The name of the sender was not on the parcel but the return address was in Kazakhstan. The parcel weighed exactly one kilogram, the maximum weight allowed by the postal service, and it contained 10 hessian bags, each with 100 grams of sugar, salt, flour, dried fruit and other food items. My aunt burst into tears, immediately realising that it was from my mother and that she was communicating that she was alive and that she had plenty to eat. She did not want us to worry. This was later confirmed in a postcard that mum was able to send us. It was wonderful to know my mother was alive, though we still knew nothing of my father's fate. It felt as though a ray of sunshine had penetrated my being. The news filled me with the secret hope that we would all be reunited and live together, once again, as a happy family.

By 1938, the purges were tapering off but my uncle could not reclaim his job because he was still uncertain about the work environment and concerned that he would be dobbed in as a traitor. Meanwhile I was having my own issues with the secret police. During Stalin's reign of terror, children of 'enemies of the people' were often placed in orphanages and given new names and identities. Almost every week, uniformed agents carrying guns in their holsters would corner me in the playground. My stomach would tighten as I watched them approach, their polished boots shining like mirrors. The conversation would always be the same: they would ask if I was being looked after properly and I would reply, "Yes, you can see I am dressed well". They would say, "Why don't you come with us?" Knowing they would take me to an orphanage I would say, "No, I must stay with my parents". In private, I would refer to Max and Rosa as my aunty and uncle but, in public, I knew to always refer to them as my mother and father. To get away, I would point to our apartment window and say, "My mother is there now, calling me in". Finally, they would let me pass.

To make matters worse, I had to keep these interactions to myself. I was too worried about the repercussions of sharing details with Max and Rosa. The situation at home was already tense and I did not want to be a burden; I was intent on protecting everyone from further worry.

We carried small red identity cards everywhere and censorship was very strict – we were only allowed to go to films deemed appropriate for our age. The cinema was far away from our apartment but my aunty did take me to see one film when she had time out from her tutoring. It reminded me of the time my mother had taken me to see a silent Charlie Chaplin film in Leningrad.

Religion did not play a role in communist Russia – Stalin was meant to be our god. Although Judaism was not part of our daily lives, I recall the time my aunt went to a play at the Shalom

Aleichem Yiddish theatre. She had puffy eyes the next day because she cried throughout the production. One day the maid took me to what I believe was the first church to open in Moscow. I remember the strong smell from the swinging incense burner made me feel sick. The whole experience was too confronting and I ran outside for fresh air.

My uncle had a huge library of first edition Russian classics that filled him with pride. He encouraged me to read works by Russian writers such as Lermontov and Pushkin, which inspired a life-long love of reading. However, my uncle made sure I read age-appropriate books and he forbade me from reading Tolstoy when I was first tempted to read the great Russian author at the age of eight.

Of course, I missed my parents terribly, particularly my father. I would replay the night he was taken away from us over and over in my mind. I was plagued by the irrational belief that everything might have turned out differently if only I had been awake that night. At the very least, I would have been able to say goodbye. But so many children had a similar story and, as a child, you live for each day. I was much older when I was able to truly comprehend how the pain of separation had seared my soul.

My uncle Sam

HERO

Once a month, my uncle Sam sent a postcard – open so the censors could read it – from Uzbekistan. Sam had an engineering degree but he wrote that he was working as a mechanic and that he had become engaged to a Russian lady called Valerie. I remember meeting his fiancée in the autumn of 1938 when she came to Moscow on her way to Uzbekistan. But, by the time she arrived, Sam had been sent to a Gulag above the Arctic Circle. Perhaps he had said the wrong thing to someone – it did not take much to upset the authorities.

On the way to the Gulag, Sam dropped a letter out of the window of the cattle truck. It said words to the effect: "Whoever finds this letter, please send it to my sister Rosa at her address in Moscow and let her know I am on the way to a Gulag". Unbelievably, someone did find the letter and, as requested, sent it on to us. We were of course distressed to hear the news and gravely concerned about how he would withstand the shocking conditions in the forced-labour camp.

Uncle Sam in Gulag, 1940

Later we received a photo of Sam from a man who had lived in the same building as us in Leningrad and who was now working as a postmaster in the Gulag. In the photo, Sam's legs are stretched out and there are crutches next to him suggesting he had been tortured. A few years later, on 20 February 1942 (I recall the date because it was my father's birthday), we received a postcard from someone stating that Sam had passed away. The postmaster also wrote to us confirming that Sam had died in the Gulag.

I had adored my uncle; he was the hero who had saved my life. I was devastated.

TIME TO LEAVE

On 23 August 1939, Stalin and Soviet foreign minister Molotov, together with Nazi foreign minister Ribbentrop, signed the German-Soviet Non-Aggression Pact in which the two countries agreed to take no military action against each other for the next 10 years. The following week, Germany invaded Poland and, two days later, France and Britain declared war on Germany, signalling the start of World War II. News of political tension in Europe was reported in the Soviet Union but it was impossible to know what was true. After a diet of propaganda, Max and Rosa were justifiably cynical of the Soviet press and found it impossible to believe the shocking reports of Nazi aggression. They certainly did not want to believe in the veracity of the reports, but it was impossible not to hold grave hopes for family members who remained in France, Germany and Poland. Communication was impossible and we had no choice but to remain optimistic about the health and safety of our extended family.

The ostensibly cordial relations between the two mighty nations who were signatories to the non-aggression pact ended on

22 June 1941 when, under the codename Operation Barbarossa, Nazi Germany invaded the Soviet Union in the largest German military operation of World War II. At the time, I was staying in a summerhouse not far from Moscow with a friend and her family. We returned to Moscow immediately. My aunt was very upset. Memories of World War I were still fresh in her mind and she was hysterical at the thought of my uncle being drafted.

By September 1941, the front was advancing nearer to Moscow and the authorities started to evacuate women and children. My aunt decided that it was time to leave and that we should finally be reunited with my mother in Kazakhstan. My uncle would follow a few months later.

The night before our departure, I went to say goodbye to my friend Zorya and other 11-year-old friends who lived in the next block. As it was getting dark, I headed towards home where I found two secret policemen standing on either side of the entrance of our building. "Where are you going?" they asked. I said, "We are going to Kazakhstan because we have been told to evacuate".

"Why? Are you going to see your mother? She is a traitor."

"No," I lied. Just then my aunt opened the curtain. "That's my mother," I said, pointing, and walked slowly past them to the relative safety of our apartment. I never ran; I knew not to show that I was afraid. And I never told anyone what happened, as we all knew that the walls had ears.[1]

---

1 I shared this story for the first time in 1967 when I was reunited with Sonia.

*My mother six months after being
released from jail in Kazakhstan*

NOWHERE

The journey to Kazakhstan in Central Asia lasted 14 gruelling days by train. Finally, in mid-October 1941, Rosa, Sonia and I arrived in the small desert village of Novvy Put. We were officially in the middle of nowhere, but at least I was finally able to reunite with my mother.

I remember the reunion as though it was yesterday. Tears of joy streamed down our faces and I basked in the warmth that radiated from my mother. I knew deep in my heart that I would probably never see my father again, but I had yearned to be held in my mother's arms and that moment had finally come.

Four years earlier, my mother had been transported to Kazakhstan along with 80 other detained women from Leningrad whose husbands had all been arrested. The population of Novyy Put was mostly comprised of people who had been forcibly displaced by the Soviets, including: Ukrainian peasants who had refused to give up their land; Kurds; and Armenians who had previously escaped from Turkey to Odessa. There were also a number of Volga Germans in the village who were the most industrious and prosperous members of this makeshift society. At the top of the unofficial hierarchy sat the Russians, followed by the Kazakhstani locals. Food scarcity was the biggest threat to the population and hunger did not discriminate; people everywhere were dying of starvation. The extreme heat in summer and unforgiving cold in winter was also responsible for many deaths.

The local people were Muslims but the open practise of religion was frowned upon and there were no mosques or other places of worship in open view. Everyone kept their faith to themselves and all religious holidays were celebrated behind closed doors and drawn curtains.

My mother was technically still in custody and was required to report to the police at the end of each week. For the first few years, that meant she reported every six days because the Soviet revolutionary calendar – created in 1929 as an anti-religious measure to banish Sunday as a day of rest – was still in force.[1]

By October 1941, the Soviets had suffered severe defeats in several battles west of Moscow and more than 600,000 Red Army soldiers had been killed or captured. Fewer than 100,000 troops remained to defend Moscow and preparations were being made to move the government east to Kuibyshev on the Volga River. As the German forces neared Moscow there was, of course, panic amongst the remaining civilians and my uncle Max was one of the many thousands who fled the city. I do not know what path he took but Max managed to make his way towards us, finally turning up on our doorstep in December. I had been so afraid of losing Max after the loss of my father and Sam. We greeted him with great joy and overwhelming relief.

Prior to our arrival in Kazakhstan, my mother had been living with a man called Leon Bogdanavich. At the time, I did not

---

1 The seven-day week was restored in 1940.

understand the nature of their relationship; I only knew that
his departure from the house made it easier for the rest of us to
squeeze in. The house, built with mud, cow dung and straw, was
not a home in any sense that I had ever known. It was very basic
and freezing cold, particularly during that first brutal winter when
temperatures dipped to negative 35 degrees. There was a fireplace
but no wood; timber was hard to come by in the desert and very
expensive. We had to make do with burning the dried grass and
leaves we managed to gather. Luckily, we were able to dress
warmly; my mother would alter heavy old clothes to fit us and my
aunt knitted us woollen gloves and socks.

Max quickly realised that there were limited opportunities
for his family in the village. He and Rosa decided to move to a
city in Uzbekistan where there was a university, in the hope that
he might find a teaching position and a good high school for
Sonia. My mother was still a prisoner serving her sentence in the
community and it was impossible for us to join them. That was
the explanation given at the time but perhaps there were other
factors in play – perhaps Max and Rosa left because I had become
so attached to them that I was struggling to reconnect with my
mother or perhaps my mother drove them away. Either way, in
March 1942, the family left the village. After being a part of their
family unit for so many years, the separation was very difficult for
me. Unbeknownst to me, that was the last time I would ever see
Max and Rosa.

I was bereft when they left, and my devastation deepened
the chasm between my mother and me. The four years that we
had been apart had taken their toll and we viewed each other with
some suspicion and disappointment. I was not the child she had
known – I had become more obstinate and independent – while

she had become a shadow of her former self, worn down from imprisonment and hard labour, scared of the dark and wary of strangers. My mother had forgotten how to be maternal and our relationship was suffused with an unspoken sadness.

After their departure, my mother's 'friend' moved back into our small house. Perhaps it was at that point that I realised my mother had lost all hope that my father was still alive. We seldom spoke about him.

Leon had never married and had no children of his own but, a few months later, his mother and niece showed up and moved in with us. I got along well with Leon and his niece but his mother resented our presence in the tiny home. It was not going to work. Mum and I moved out and found lodgings with a Jewish Polish family. By then, the Soviets had started deporting people from Russian-occupied Poland to Gulags in Siberia and to countries in Central Asia including Kazakhstan. It was crowded in the two-room dwelling but as a child you take it as it comes; we were all refugees after all.

I started attending school but I did not have any books or writing materials, so a little girl who befriended me took me to a 'shop'. Coming from Moscow, where I had access to so many beautiful books, I was shocked to see that the only items on the shelf were three exercise books and a few pencils. I exclaimed, "There's nothing here!" The Russian lieutenant in uniform standing behind me said, "What do you mean? Look! There are exercise books and pencils". I immediately realised my mistake and said, "One book would be nice thank you".

Everything was ideologically controlled from the party down and we were all still pretending to be good communists. My mother was friends with a Jewish woman from Leningrad who made a living taking photos at funerals. She would photograph family members standing around an open coffin. She said they were the easiest portraits to take because, without any encouragement, everyone would stand very still and no one was expected to smile. The woman was twice widowed and, on the wall in her home, she had two photos of her family congregating around the coffins of her dead husbands, which I remember finding bizarre. Between the two photos was a portrait of Stalin – a ruse to convince the authorities that she remained a faithful devotee of the ruthless Soviet dictator. I realised that nothing could be further from the truth when, one night, she read to me from old journals printed during the czar's time, pre-revolution. She swore me to secrecy. If someone found those forbidden anti-communist journals she would have been arrested.

My mother and I were struggling. There was no time for fun, there was only survival. We eventually found a new place for the two of us to live alone but there was no running water, so each morning I would walk along the icy path to get water from the well, which I would carry home in two buckets attached to a piece of wood balanced behind my neck. There was no toilet so we would do our business in a nearby field and, without electricity, we were dependent on our oil burner and candles for light. My mother continued to work every day in the fields at the *kolhotz*[2] but her monthly wage barely lasted us a day so, for sustenance, we were dependent on our daily ration of 100 grams of bread. I would queue for hours to collect the small, heavy slabs of bread, which looked like pumpernickel but were not as tasty.

In the summer of 1943, while temperatures in the desert soared to 45 degrees, my mother contracted tropical malaria. The fever lasted five days and I had to nurse her while she repeated

---

2 A *kolhotz* is a collective farm.

over and over, "I don't want to die here". Thankfully there was a doctor amongst the Leningrad women who gave her a certificate saying she was unfit to work. It was just before the expiration of her sentence so she was excused from working at the *kolhotz* and never went back.

Not long afterwards, I contracted typhoid fever. I was hospitalised but, due to overcrowding and a delousing program at the hospital, my bed was on the floor of the laundry. After four weeks, I was allowed to go home and I remember begging my mother for a piece of bread. She was concerned that it would be too hard to digest after so many weeks of soft food but eventually I wore her down and she gave me some. It was a mistake; my intestines had become so thin that I suffered terrible abdominal pain and was readmitted to hospital. In all, I missed four months of school so I was moved down to the lower class. That was very demoralising for me. I was not coping so, at the age of 13, I left school. That was the end of my formal education. I rationalised that my time was best spent working or looking for food so that we had enough to eat.

My mother did not try to convince me to stay at school. By then she was physically and mentally depleted, overwhelmed by all that had happened to her in the previous few years: her imprisonment, the trauma of not knowing what had happened to her husband, the isolation, and the dire state of our current situation. From the age of seven to 11, I had become used to life in a new family unit and I had developed a strong and wilful nature. Meanwhile, during that four-year period my mother had not known if I was alive. We were never able to bridge the gap and we became estranged, which is something I have always regretted. My mother and I looked after each other as best we could, but it was a burden to me that I was not able to give my mother the love and attention that she craved.

Whenever we were behind in the rent, we were forced to move. At one stage we were living with the Kurds – which was as low as you could go – but then we managed to secure a house with a small plot of land. Finally, we could keep chickens and goats and grow our own food. However, watering the radish, cucumber and tomato plants required ingenuity and strength. Using water from the nearby river for private plots of land was considered stealing so the villagers established a secret irrigation system that could only be turned on at night. The problem was that the small water canals had to be diverted to reach each individual plot. During that period, a lot of injured soldiers were returning to their families. Despite their injuries, the soldiers were stronger than me and would change the canals to flow back towards their own land. Watering our plot was like playing a secret game of tug of war.

That year was the worst for us. Without any income, we were forced to sell all our personal belongings. But my mother refused to sell our most prized possessions: three large and two small goats. Each morning as the sun rose, a shepherd would come and take the goats out to the pastures in exchange for a small fee or food. He would bring them back by sunset so that I could milk them. I carefully guarded those goats – they were our fortune.

Our house had a large oven in the middle of the only room and during winter we would put our beds on top of the oven to keep warm. It was my job to ensure that there was enough coal clustered in the corner of the oven to smoulder all night. I had a special metal dish and I would knock on the neighbours' doors and ask for hot coal. Sometimes people would come to us for the same thing. Everyone helped when they could; we were all in the same situation after all. I had one treasured book that I had brought with me from Moscow. It was a beautiful German edition of Shakespeare. I was devastated one night when, out of desperation, I had to tear out the pages to get the fire going.

Lack of hygiene was an ongoing problem as there was limited clean water and no sewerage, so people were forced to relieve themselves outside. After living in Moscow, I was continually shocked by the primitive conditions in our town, which seemed far worse than even the other villages nearby. I remember watching a Kazakhstani woman scratching her head and then biting something. I asked my mother what she was doing and she said the woman probably had lice. Apparently, the local people believed in biting back whatever had bitten them!

In May 1944, after many bloody battles on the Eastern Front, the Red Army liberated German-held Crimea.[3] In another deliberate act of ethnic cleansing, the Soviets then exiled the Crimean Tatars as collective punishment for those accused of being Nazi collaborators. Thousands of Crimean Tatars, including women and children, were transported in cattle trucks to Uzbekistan. At various times we saw many hundreds of people walking through the desert, being herded like cattle along the main road. They would beg for a drink and I would run to them carrying our enamel jug filled with water. Watching all those poor people walking without hope made a terrible impression on me – I would think about my father and despair over his unknown fate.

One day when I was trying to make some money, I sold my suitcase to the lady who ran the bakery. She could see from the condition of the suitcase that I had come from a more affluent world. We started talking and she took pity on me. She gave me bread and said I should regularly come to collect bread from her.

---

3 These battles were known as the Crimean Offensive.

Crimean Tatars being herded through the desert, 1944

She became a friend to me at a particularly difficult period of
my life.

When my mother finished serving her sentence, she was
given a Russian passport that stated she had been a political
prisoner for five years. The number 53 was printed in her passport
to signify the nature of her alleged crimes. Technically we were
allowed to travel again but she was to be forever branded
a criminal.

Now that she was 'free', my mother secured a job in a small
factory that produced grey jackets with quilted down for the army.
At the factory, my mother met a Polish tailor who helped her get
a clean passport. He made the arrangements behind the scenes
but it fell to me to take the money and collect the documents
from the secretary of the commissar who issued the papers. As
I was not yet 16, I did not need my own passport; my mother's
passport included all my identification details, including the false
information that I was born in Warsaw. There were no documents
to prove otherwise and it was not a good time to declare that you
were born in Germany.

It was the summer of 1944 and the Soviet Union was winning
the war. It was finally safe for my uncle and aunt to go back to
Moscow. Despite now having a clean passport, because of my
mother's 'criminal record', we still were not allowed within a
200-kilometre radius of any major city. Our secret plan was to get
out of the Soviet Union altogether but, not knowing if that was
possible, we decided to get as close to a border as we could. Of
course, we could not share that information with anyone without
risking our lives so we told everyone we were going to a city about
200 kilometres west of Moscow called Yaroslavl to be as near as
possible to our family.

We had very few personal possessions left but finally it was time to sell the goats; we exchanged them for a few thousand rubles, enough money to see us through the next few months. Those goats were our saviours. We packed two sets of clothing for each season into hessian bags that we carried over our shoulders and, after saying goodbye to our few remaining friends, we left the village.

____

HEADING WEST

We travelled in cattle trucks in a westerly direction towards Europe. We had no real destination in mind – our only thought was to get out of the Soviet Union. We had Mum's passport and we thought there might be a chance we could cross the border and find our family in Poland and France.

Of course we had heard about the terrible atrocities being committed by the Germans but we did not believe the stories. My mother said it was Russian propaganda. I remember her saying, "That can't be true. That does not sound like the Germans I grew up with". It was beyond our comprehension that such evil could be a reality but, as we travelled through the Ukraine, we became filled with a sense of dread. Along one 800-kilometre stretch near Kiev, we did not see a single human, cow, dog or cat. Nothing. The Germans had razed the whole region. A once-thriving countryside had become a wasteland.

I remember feeling particularly scared when our train travelled over a bridge near the town of Donetsk. The bridge had been partially destroyed and hastily fixed so the train had to move at a snail's pace so as not to damage the weakened structure. I was terrified that we would fall into the river below.

The journey was long because we had to make our way around the Caspian Sea, and we became increasingly anxious as we approached the frontline. We had no idea how long we would be allowed to keep moving forward. For four harrowing weeks we lived on those cattle trains without seats, and at every station we would fill our little steel basin with boiling water to wash our clothes on the platform. To make money along the way, we would buy food at one station and sell it at the next one, counting on the rumours that there were shortages of certain items including herring, salt and apples.

We did not intend to go to Rovno in the Ukraine but that was as far west as we were allowed to travel. The war was raging 200 kilometres away and only soldiers were allowed to remain on board the cattle truck. Rovno was the last station for civilians and we all had to get off. My mother told me to stay on the platform with our possessions while she looked around. She came back crying and exclaiming, "What have we done? We have jumped from the frying pan into the fire". She had seen hundreds of people walking, holding bags and carrying children. The stationmaster explained that they were leaving town to hide in the woods. With the Germans so close, there was a real fear that the town was about to be bombed.

By then it was almost dark and a curfew was in place. We had nowhere to go so we decided to sleep at the station. We used the toilet, sponged ourselves clean with hot running water, put on a pair of clean underwear and finally fell into a fitful sleep on the cold concrete platform. Luckily it was summer.

The next morning, we woke to the sight of a well-dressed man laying *tefillin* on the platform. I had never seen the small black prayer boxes before and I asked my mother what he was doing. My mother told me to keep quiet and let him finish. When the man finished praying, she approached him and apologised for disturbing him. She explained our situation and told him that we wanted to go to Poland to find our family. From the expression on his face, it started to sink in that our plan was ludicrous.

The religious man told us to go to the bazaar. He said that it was a big market day and that we would find a man called Mr Melamed who was helping all the Jews arriving in Rovno. He said to look for a small man with bow legs and a heart of gold. Mr Melamed would approach anyone who looked Jewish or any lost soul.

We found Mr Melamed in the market and he located a spare room for us in the home of a young Czech couple. There was a Czech colony in Rovno and the Czech people were extremely industrious and wonderful to the Jews at their own peril. Mr Melamed said that once we were settled, he would find us something more permanent. In the meantime, he told us to go straight to the police station to register our new address so that my mother could find work. Otherwise, he warned, the town authorities would expel us from Rovno and we would be forced to retreat to the village outside town where partisans were fighting against the Russians to free the Ukraine. The partisans were collaborating with the Germans so, as Jews, we would surely be killed. He assured us that, despite the threat of bombings, we would be safest in Rovno where there was a large Russian military and police presence.

My mother quickly secured a job as a secretary in a shoe factory and I started school. It soon became clear that we could not survive on her pitiful salary of 120 rubles per month and, because the school was so far away, I had no time to earn money after my classes. So, once again, I quit school to ensure we had enough money to eat. My mother was not happy, but what choice did we have? Winter was coming and we only had the clothes on our backs. Mr Melamed introduced us to a lady who could give me cigarette papers and sewing cotton on credit and I started selling the goods at the large open-air bazaar. I did not have my own stand but a Jewish lady with similar merchandise said I could sell next to her.

We scrapped together a living that allowed us to pay rent for our room. I was so happy to be able to purchase delicious loaves of bread and butter from huge bowls at the bazaar. After some time, we even managed to buy a sewing machine so that we could be decently dressed.

In the bazaar there were loudspeakers and my mother and her workmates would come during their lunch break to hear the news. Still, my mother refused to believe what she was hearing about the brutality of the Germans and the decimation of the Jews. She simply could not reconcile revelations about the Nazi atrocities with the German people she had known during her childhood.

HIDING

In the factory where Mum worked there was a small, dingy kitchen that no one used. Mum decided that, to save money, we should move our few belongings into the kitchen and sleep there each night. She assured me that there was a huge table in the kitchen that we could use as a bed base. So we moved out of the house and into the factory. Of course, it had to be done in secret. Each morning we would hide our belongings and I would leave before the workers arrived. Our situation was far from ideal but we had become accustomed to living in squalid conditions. We were safe as long as no one discovered our secret.

Things were fine until a new director started at the factory. He had his eye on my mother but, after she rejected his advances, he began tormenting her. He must have been suspicious because he arrived early one day and found us asleep on the kitchen table. Out of spite, he told the authorities. We were homeless again but, thankfully, my mother was allowed to keep her job.

Mr Melamed had earlier introduced us to two very nice sisters from Warsaw. My mother had become friendly with them and she told them the whole story in the hope that they could help us find accommodation. The sisters introduced us to a lovely Czech family who had a house in the centre of town in a street named Berlinski. They took us in and we were allocated two rooms: a bedroom with a kitchenette and a little cellar. We had no running water but there was a pump across the street. It was a big improvement.

The two sisters asked if we could hide a young Jewish couple who were on the run from the secret police. Mum said no, it was too risky. We were as afraid of the Russians as the Germans and Poles, and there was a Russian lieutenant living next door. I was still petrified of the secret police and I always made detours to avoid them. Despite this fear, behind my mother's back, I agreed to hide the couple in the dark, dingy cellar overnight until they could be moved to the next safe house. I never told my mother I had hidden them there and I still regret deceiving her in that way.

END OF THE WAR

became friendly with a Ukrainian girl whose mother was the
inspector at the market. One day, my friend told me she had
access to salt that she could give me on consignment to sell at the
market. Salt was in high demand because pickled vegetables were
such an important part of an Eastern European diet. So I added salt
to my stock at the stall and it sold well. Each afternoon I would go
to my friend's house to give her some money and pick up the next
day's supply. I had no idea who was supplying her with all this
salt; it was best to never ask questions.

After the market one day in May 1945, I went to my friend's
house as usual. Suddenly we could hear shooting, so we looked
out the window to see Cossacks galloping around on their horses,
shooting into the air. We had no idea what was happening.

At that moment, my friend's mother ran in to tell us that the
woman who lived downstairs had gone into labour and we had
to help her get to the hospital. The next few hours were chaotic.
Somehow, the three of us managed to carry the screaming pregnant
woman to the hospital while all around us people were shooting

and shouting in the street. It was only once we arrived at the hospital that we discovered the noise was the sound of jubilation: the war was over.

I arrived home hours later to find my mother in a highly agitated state. When I had failed to arrive home on time, my mother had managed to overcome her fear of the dark to walk through the crowded streets to the inspector's house. When she could not find me, she ran home, terrified that something terrible had happened.

Thinking she would calm down when she heard how we had heroically helped a pregnant woman, I told her about the night's events and shared the incredible news that the war was over. Instead, she became hysterical and started thrashing me with her hairbrush. Her traumatic walk and fear that I had been killed, mixed with her relief that the war was finally over had been intense enough; but hearing me utter the taboo words 'pregnant' and 'birth' sent her over the edge. I really got a beating. What should have been a night of celebration became a night of terror and despair. It was the only time she ever hit me; I stood there and took it.

At the time, I could not understand her reaction. In fact, I had not been able to relate to my mother for a very long time. I searched for, but never found, the warm person I had known when I was seven. In the years after our reunion, our relationship was marred by the turmoil in our lives. She was damaged. But I did not fully realise it at the time.

RETURNING

News started trickling in about the concentration camps in Europe but my mother still refused to accept the Russian reports. She simply could not believe it. We clung to the desperate hope that my father's family was still alive in Lodz and that my mother's family had survived the war in Paris. Above all, we hoped against all hope that my father was still alive.

Meanwhile Russian 'justice' in Soviet-occupied Ukraine was still a frightening reality. During the winter of 1945, the Soviet authorities rounded up everyone working in the bazaar and forced us to watch as they hung eight men – one by one – in the open area of the marketplace. It was a compulsory lesson for the local population: this is what happens if you fight underground against the Russian state. The eight men were supposedly members of the Organisation of Ukrainian Nationalists fighting for independence. The final man to be executed had the last word: as they put the noose around his neck he called out, "Long live Bandera".[1] Whether the other men were really members of that group or just guilty by association was impossible to know. The hanging was so

---

1 Stepan Bandera was a Ukrainian political activist and leader
   of the independence movement in the 1940s.

graphic, so grotesque, my 15-year-old brain could hardly process what I was witnessing.

Soldiers returning from the war sold their army uniforms at the bazaar. We could not afford a heavy green officer's uniform so we bought one of the basic grey uniforms. The wool was not as soft but it was warm and that was the important thing. My mother turned the uniform into a coat that helped me survive the brutal winter.

A few Jewish survivors returned to Rovno after the war to search for family and to reclaim their homes and businesses. One Jewish man reopened his bakery and, during Passover, he started making matzah. My mother and I tasted the dry unleavened bread but it was awful and held no cultural significance for us; we preferred bread. I became friendly with one young Jewish woman with a heart of gold who was the only surviving member of her family. She was very pretty but cross-eyed and the children in the town teased her mercilessly. One day my friend showed me around the one remaining synagogue in town. She introduced me to the local *shochet*[1] and explained the koshering of meat. The day before Passover, we heard that the secret police had come for the *shochet*. The rumour was that he had been buying and selling Russian gold coins dating from the last czar, which was prohibited because all the gold was meant to be stored in the treasury. Reportedly, the *shochet* had seen the police coming, jumped the fence and disappeared. This caused much consternation for the religious people of the town, including my lovely friend. She approached me at the market and told me that she had a live chicken but did not know how to kill it. Would I do it for her? She knew I had killed chickens before and that I was Jewish. That would have to suffice. So, I killed the chicken for her. But really, what did I know about kosher food?

____

2 Jewish butcher responsible for slaughtering animals in
accordance with kosher guidelines.

From the time the war ended, we wanted to leave Rovno but it was not easy to arrange and we did not have any money. However, as the post-war chaos subsided, authorities began to systematically deport Polish citizens back to Poland. In order to leave, you needed a document from your workplace to show that your tax payments were up to date, and of course you had to provide evidence of citizenship. Our Polish contacts signed my mother's documents to declare that they had known her before the war in Warsaw; she had actually been in Germany before the war but because she was born in Warsaw it was partially true. Fortunately, I was on my mother's passport so I was officially a Polish citizen too. Anything was better than saying you were born in Germany. The problem was that the director of the factory did not want to provide proof that she owed no taxes to the state.

One day we heard a rumour that cattle trucks were coming to transport Polish citizens home. We packed and prepared to go to the station at a moment's notice. But first we had to get our documents stamped, so I ran to the station and, with my small hand, I slid my mother's passport between two large women at the front of the queue. The Russians were not checking the documents properly; they just stamped every piece of paper in front of them. Even though I had not produced the tax document, we had the stamp we needed. I ran to the factory and said, "Mum, we are going". The director was furious, complaining, "I didn't give you permission!" But it did not matter – Mum's passport had been stamped and we were ready to leave.

We went to the station with all our belongings in hessian bags and our most treasured possession: a 10-litre milk can filled with vodka to sell on the journey. We carried it in an upside-stool so that it would not tilt and spill. Finally, we boarded a cattle train along with hundreds of Polish refugees heading back to what had once been their home.

On the train we connected with the cousin of the fellow who had arranged my mother's clean passport in Kazakhstan. He told us that his cousin was already in Poland and that he had settled in the coalmining town of Bytom. The man warned us that we were unlikely to find our family in Lodz but that if we went to Bytom his cousin would help us.

By that time, we were starting to believe the horrifying stories of the systematic murder of millions of Jews. We could see the devastation and at each station we got off to make enquiries. People told us that the reality was worse than we could ever imagine. Everyone said there were no Jews left at all. Some asked us bluntly, "How are you still alive?"

After 10 weary days of travel, we arrived at the station at Bytom in southern Poland. With growing despair, my mother said, "Let's stop here; at least we know someone here who is still alive". There were vacant homes all over the town because so many Jewish Poles had been killed and the Nazis who had lived in Bytom during the war had all retreated. A few Jewish survivors who had returned to the town told us about one particular house for homeless people where we found an empty room with a small oven. We were squatters. We were surprised to find a suitcase in the wardrobe that was filled with bundles of German money but, instead of being overjoyed by our find, we wrongly assumed the currency was no longer valid and we burned most of it to keep ourselves warm as winter set in. To make matters worse, a few months later my mother hid $100 that we had saved in zlotys and exchanged into US dollars. She hid the money somewhere in the building and never found it again.

Presumably it was discovered and taken by another tenant. I was very upset. That was our fortune.

No one could tell what nationality I was: I was blonde and blue-eyed but neither Russian nor Ukrainian. I spoke a bit of Polish learned during our time in Rovno, but not enough to pass as Polish. I tried to settle in as best I could but my mother was a broken woman, forced to start over yet again.

I continued the work of buying stock and selling it at the market. One day a woman approached me at the bazaar and said she recognised me from Kazakhstan. I told her she was mistaken. I did not want anything to do with that chapter of my life; I wanted to completely disassociate myself from the past.

Jewish people continued to return from the liberated concentration camps as well as from the Soviet Union. At first there was little infrastructure to assist Jewish survivors but, over time, welfare agencies began to emerge. One Jewish agency took possession of the house where we were staying because the owners had not returned, and we were allowed to continue living in our room on the second floor.

We heard from these survivors that the Lodz ghetto had been liquidated and that everyone living there had been sent to Auschwitz. We knew that in 1941 my father's family had been detained in the Lodz ghetto because my aunt Bertha had a nanny who wrote to our cousins in New York to advise them about the development. The nanny had thrown bread over the fence to the family whenever possible. Upon hearing the news about the ghetto, our hopes of finding my father or anyone in his family completely disappeared.

At no point did we consider going back to Russia. Apart from the fact that we were not allowed, the news from Moscow was not

encouraging: Sonia was studying medicine and my uncle Max was
working but Rosa was very sick and they were living in a one-room
apartment with a communal kitchen. Everything was rationed and
life was tough. New people had settled into their apartment and
taken possession of all their belongings, including the furniture
and rugs. The only things they had not wanted were the books;
I was pleased that, at least, my uncle had his prized library.

My mother and her brother Max remained hopeful that
their family had managed to survive in Paris. They had no way to
discover their fate, however, as neither Max nor my mother could
recall their parents' last known address.

On my 16th birthday

ZIONISM

A Zionist youth movement called Hashomer Hatzair was preparing about 30 young Jewish people to migrate to Palestine.[1] I was excited about the possibility of leaving Europe so I joined the movement and moved into their boarding house near our lodgings. My mother did not try to stop me – not that she had any control over me by then.

At 16, I was the youngest person in the movement. Our days were divided into household chores and lessons about culture and history. The leaders also tried to teach us Hebrew. Still imbued with the anti-religious Russian way of thinking, I resisted learning what I considered to be the language of the bible. Only two of us in the youth movement had come out of Russia – myself and a man who had been born and raised in Poland in a family with Jewish traditions. Everyone at the house spoke Yiddish so I mostly relied on my German language skills and, occasionally, that young man would translate my Russian into Polish. I still knew so little about being Jewish and the whole experience of living with other Jewish people was very strange. The language, customs and age barriers

---

1 The State of Israel was not created until 1948. The Hashomer Hatzair movement organised illegal immigration of Jewish refugees to Palestine. Many members were also involved in the Haganah military movement.

made the experience particularly challenging but everyone was kind to each other. I was one of the lucky few who had a parent alive, almost everyone else had been orphaned during the war. The ones who had come from camps did not talk much about their experiences – everyone was trying to focus on the future.

During that period, I made friends with two sisters aged 24 and 26. They did not belong to the movement but were sent from Jewish Welfare to visit me. They had survived the war hidden by Polish people until it became too dangerous and they joined the partisans.

After a few months, we amalgamated with another Jewish youth group and moved to a large, clean dormitory in the town of Sosnowiec 20 kilometres away. My mother stayed in Bytom but travelled by tram to visit me occasionally. Then we moved again, this time to the town of Katowice, which was only 10 kilometres from Bytom, so I could visit my mother more regularly.

One day it was my turn to be on cooking duty. The budget was tight so we tended to eat a lot of noodles. My mother was visiting and I became distracted and burned the noodles. I remember she suggested I soak them in water and then recook them with sauce and thankfully no one seemed to notice. Whatever we had to eat was more than we were used to – we had all experienced starvation during the war years. We were particularly grateful to have vegetables, especially carrots, and sometimes even fruit such as apples and pears.

I did not know what to think of the idea of moving to Palestine but we were being indoctrinated. I remember watching people doing the *hora* and learning songs in Hebrew. I would sing along without understanding the meaning.

One day when I was in Katowice, my mother woke up from a deep sleep with a clear memory of her parents' address in Paris.

Unbeknownst to me, she wrote to her family and was thrilled, after several weeks, to finally receive a telegram. She came to tell me the joyful news we had been waiting so long to hear: her parents – my grandparents – were alive, and so was her sister Jenny and her family. They had survived.

With a friend, 1946

RESISTANCE

When my maternal grandmother first moved to Paris in 1933, she became friendly with the concierge in their apartment building. They lived at 22 Rue Richer close to the celebrated Folies Bergère music hall.

In 1942, when Paris was no longer safe for Jewish people, the concierge hid my grandparents in one of the building's 12 attics. They were effectively prisoners but they could walk around in socks and whisper quietly. The concierge used a secret knock to bring them water and whatever food she could spare; she would also remove their waste.

One day, after nine months, an SS officer turned up at the building and asked the concierge if she was hiding anyone. There was a rumour, he said, that she was harbouring Jews in an attic. The concierge invited the SS officer to inspect the attics, showing him an empty attic on the right side of the stairwell first. The attic was particularly dusty and the Nazi started to cough. When the concierge offered to show him another attic, he said that would not be necessary and he ran out to get some fresh air.

That night, the concierge entered the attic and said to my grandmother, "Carola, I am sad to say I can't keep you here any longer – one or two more nights at the most. Please pack your belongings, I have arranged for you to go to Grenoble". Grenoble was the town in south-east France at the foot of the Alps where my aunt Jenny and uncle Nathan Lewenberg were living with their daughter Miriam (Mira) and newborn baby Suzanne (Susie). Nathan was a Turkish citizen and, before Germany invaded France, he had managed to secure false non-Jewish papers for his family so they could live in relative safety.

Luckily for my grandparents, the concierge had a brother – or perhaps it was a cousin – who by day was a clerk working for the Vichy French government and by night was working in the resistance. He arranged false identification papers for my grandparents and, one night, he used the special knock and quietly told them, "Don't worry. Follow me. Walk softly". Together, they crept down the six flights of stairs and entered the dark, empty street. A curfew was in place, so they had to walk in the shadows to the nearby park where another person met them; again, no names were exchanged but they were given a password to use at the next checkpoint. In this way, the resistance helped my grandparents travel the 565 kilometres to Grenoble.

My grandparents arrived in Grenoble just as Jenny and her husband were preparing to leave. It was never properly explained to me but, for some reason to do with the Italian fascists who were controlling the region, they had to flee the area, but it was safe for my grandparents to stay. They had decided to take Mira, aged four, with them but to leave their baby behind with a wet nurse. They were not sure they would be able to provide for the baby and they knew that in the countryside with her wet nurse, she would at least get milk.

Jenny gave her parents some money and told them to check on the baby from time to time. My grandmother was appalled when she saw the conditions on the farm where Susie was living. The wet nurse was a peasant woman with four children of her own, as well as cattle to look after. Without a moment's hesitation, my grandparents took the baby from the farm to stay with them in the nearby village. They all survived the war there thanks to the false papers given to them by the partisans.

In August 1944, Paris was liberated and Jenny, Nathan and Mira returned to their former home. Soon after, my grandparents also returned with Susie. There, they waited in vain for news of the rest of their family.

At the beginning of the war, despite having false papers, my mother's youngest brother, Marek, had been transported to the Drancy internment camp. The family was never certain if he was denounced as a communist or taken by mistake. Six months later, Marek's wife, Eva, also received a notice stating that she would soon be sent to Drancy. Naively, Eva hoped that at Drancy she would be reunited with her husband and she decided to take their son Ilia with her, even though he was not named in the deportation notice. My grandfather was horrified to learn that Ilia was going to Drancy and insisted that the boy remain behind with him. Later, my grandfather somehow arranged for Ilia to be sent on a transport to Switzerland where he was taken in by a Swiss couple who were determined to save Jewish children. His decisive actions saved Ilia's life. Sadly, however, Marek and Eva never returned after the war. Many years later, we learned that they were both murdered in Auschwitz.

My grandparents were not able to reclaim their apartment but secured accommodation across two attics in the building next door. When, two years later, their former concierge received a letter from my mother addressed to her parents, she decided that, rather than climbing to their attic next door, she would give it to my grandparents when she saw them next. It was three weeks before she finally handed them my mother's letter. They were, of course, overjoyed to learn that we were still alive and immediately replied by telegram.

————————————

SEEKING A HOME

Knowing that any journey to Palestine would involve travelling through France, my mother made the pragmatic decision to stick with the current plan and stay with the Zionist group. In any case, we had no money to fund our own journey.

Two days after my mother received the telegram, on 4 July 1946, a pogrom erupted in Kielce. Forty-two Jews who had survived the Holocaust were violently killed by Polish soldiers, police officers and civilians. Another 40 were wounded. The plan to leave Poland and travel to Palestine took on a new urgency.

Within days we were told that the clandestine network was in place for our journey and illegal entry into Palestine.[1] About 40 of us, including the few parents in the group, would be travelling together under the guise of Turkish refugees. I worried that my blonde hair and blue eyes would be our undoing. During a mission briefing, we were told that we would be travelling by day and sometimes through the night, mostly by train and on foot. Bribes would be used to secure passage through checkpoints and, when that was not possible, barbed wire fences would be cut and we could expect to crawl across borders.

---

1 Palestine was occupied by British forces who were refusing entry to Jewish refugees.

The first leg of our journey was by train to the border of Czechoslovakia, which was not yet under communist rule. At the border we were told by our guides to form a straight line and feel our way along the wire fence in the dark until we reached an opening. If we saw a light, we were to lie down and hide in the tall grass. We finally found the opening and entered Czechoslovakia where we were met by soldiers from the Jewish Brigade Group, a military unit of the British Army. We were then transported to Bratislava where we stayed in a building we later nicknamed 'bed bugs hotel'. A few days later we travelled by train towards Vienna and walked the last 10 kilometres of the journey to enter the city.

As far as I was concerned, we were going to Palestine but for Mum, it was a strange, winding route to her family in Paris. She handled the journey well because the goal seemed achievable and, for once, we could simply follow the rules. We were given precise instructions about how to behave: we had to remain close and we were never to speak Polish; it was important to always pretend not to understand the languages spoken around us.

As we drew close to Vienna we saw a group of drunk Russian prisoners-of-war making fun of us while they worked behind barbed wire. They were saying, "The Turks are coming" and laughing their heads off. I thought to myself, you are in a worse position than we are: the Austrian police will be after you.[1]

The Soviets had captured Austria in 1945 and formed a provisional government, but the Allies soon crossed the borders and agreed on the boundaries of four zones to be occupied by the United States, Soviet Union, United Kingdom and France. Vienna was similarly divided amongst the four nations. As soon as we arrived, we were taken to the Rothschild Hospital in the American section and I will never forget the joy of being handed a bar of soap

2 According to 1946 Austrian police records, "men in Soviet uniform", usually drunk, accounted for more than 90 per cent of registered crimes including sexual violence against women and violent interrogation of civilians.

and a towel. We remained in Vienna for a week and our minders
would let us go for walks, as long as we did not stray too far from
the hospital. My mother and I were full of admiration for the
beautiful flowers on display at a nearby florist. I had never seen
a shop selling flowers; in the Soviet Union we had only ever seen
flowers growing in the wild. I remember thinking that life must be
wonderful in Vienna.

From Austria, we were smuggled into Germany in
camouflaged army trucks. We mostly travelled at night so we did
not see anything of the bombed cities but we had seen enough of
that in the Ukraine and Poland. For several days we stayed at the
displaced persons (DP) camp in the spa town of Stuttgart. Each
morning after breakfast, we were allowed to leave the camp and
walk to the local park. As we were walking, my mother greeted
people in German. I was surprised and asked if she knew the
people she was saying hello to. She said no, it was just good
manners to say *"guten tag"* to people you saw walking in the park.

One morning, we were told that it was time to leave and that
several other Jewish refugees from the DP camp would be joining
us. We were divided into groups and given water and a piece of
bread. We were told not to expect any more food that day and to
drink very little because there would be no toilet stops. We would
be travelling in a convoy of army trucks through Switzerland into
France. Our drivers would be in uniform but we were told not to
be afraid, they were Jewish soldiers from Palestine. Whether it was
good planning or just sheer luck, we were not stopped and our
journey was uneventful.

The problem was that my mother and I were separated into
two different trucks. We were told that we would meet up at our

Stuttgart refugee barracks

destination, but instead my mother was taken to Dijon and I was taken to Marseille. I was assured that she had arrived safely and that at some point we would be reunited.

Our group was amazed to find that we were being housed in a beautiful villa near the seaside. We were excited to be in France and to be living in relative luxury. We were even allowed to swim at the beach. We were told that we would remain there for at least a week. I dutifully followed my mother's instructions: she had told me that if ever we became separated, I should write to my grandmother in Paris and tell her my whereabouts. So, I wrote that I was in Marseille in a house near the beach but that I had no idea of the address of our accommodation.

On her third day in Dijon, my mother, frustrated by her lack of freedom, pretended she was sick and in need of a doctor. Somehow, she convinced the men guarding the group that she needed to leave the accommodation and go into the town centre to seek medical attention. Wandering the streets, she noticed a jeweller who she suspected was Jewish. In her desperation, she approached the man to request his help. Her instincts were correct – he was Jewish. She said, "I have no money but I have parents and a sister in Paris. If you would be kind enough to lend me some money for a train fare, my sister will reimburse you immediately when I arrive". She gave the man her sister's address and he, understanding my mother's predicament, gave her enough money for the second-class fare and food for the journey. My mother went straight to the station and the man sent telegrams to my grandmother and Jenny notifying them that my mother would be arriving in Paris the next morning. We had been told by our leaders to destroy all our documents so it was fortunate that she could move freely within France without a passport or any other form of identification.

My grandmother received the telegram and immediately contacted my aunt who was on holiday in the countryside. Jenny took the first train back to Paris and was waiting at the station when my mother disembarked. My grandparents were waiting at Jenny's apartment when my mother walked through the door for the tearful reunion.

Somehow, through a Jewish welfare organisation, my mother found the address of the house where our group was staying and, 10 days after arriving in Marseille, she came for me. The people minding us in Marseille were Jewish soldiers in the Haganah, who had been fighting the Nazis but were now fighting to free Palestine from British rule. When my mother explained that I had to leave with her, the uniformed man became livid. He had good reason to be upset: a lot of time, energy and money had been invested in my escape. He yelled, "Get out of my sight". I remember him screaming at us as we hastily departed down the stairs. Because of me, another person had missed out on being saved.

For me, going to Palestine had only ever been a means of escape from the Soviets; the youth leaders had not succeeded in turning me into a Zionist. I was barely 16 years old and, at the time, I could not really comprehend that, for that soldier, our actions were a shocking betrayal.

Jenny with Susie (left) and Mira (right), 1946

PARIS

My uncle Nathan had managed to continue paying the rent on his parents' apartment throughout the war years, without knowing if they were still living there or even if they were still alive. When Paris was liberated, Jenny and Nathan returned to find the beautifully furnished apartment untouched and uninhabited; the breakfast dishes still sat on the table three years after the Nazis had forcibly removed his parents from their home. It was later confirmed that Nathan's parents had perished in Auschwitz, as had Nathan's brother who was captured when trying to escape to Switzerland.

Jenny decided that the family could not live in that apartment – as the memories were too painful. Instead she managed to secure a huge second-floor apartment in Rue des Anges. It was in terrible shape but they modernised the space and moved in with Mira and Susie.

When my mother and I disembarked in Paris after a sleepless journey on the overnight train, we went directly

to Jenny's apartment. It was August; everything was closed
for the holidays and the family had returned to the countryside.
My mother had the key and as soon as we entered the apartment
I fell into an exhausted sleep. My aunt arrived back that afternoon
to find me fast asleep in Susie's cot.

The next day we travelled to the countryside to meet the rest
of the family. I remember feeling nervous: I had no memory of my
grandfather and only a vague recollection of saying goodbye to my
grandmother when I was three. I was still scarred by the memory
of my paternal grandmother who had been so mean to me.

My grandmother introduced me to Mira and then to Susie
saying, "Ruth, I love you dearly but you must understand this
grandchild is special to me because I looked after her from when
she was a newborn". I did not mind that I would never be my
grandmother's favourite; I was just happy to see her.

My grandfather was kind to me but he was not a well man.
I do not recall the nature of his illness but he also suffered from
depression. He carried the deep sadness of losing his youngest son
Marek and his daughter-in-law Eva in the Holocaust.

Eva and Marek's son, Ilia, survived the war in Switzerland
and his foster parents had been keen to adopt him. They said
they would treat him as their own son and that, out of respect to
his Jewish heritage, they would ensure he had religious tuition.
My grandparents refused and insisted that Ilia return to France.
As a concession, they allowed Ilia to visit the couple during the
holidays. Then, because they were still living in the two attics,
my grandparents made the strange decision to put Ilia into a
communist orphanage and, later, into a religious children's home.
Poor Ilia hated it there and would often run away to Jenny's

apartment. He would time his escape with the start of *Shabbat* so that he could not be returned until after sundown on the Saturday. Later, it would regularly fall on me to return Ilia to the children's home whenever he ran away. It always seemed terribly unjust to me that no one in our family had the means or desire to look after him. Many years later Ilia told me he would have loved to be adopted by the Swiss couple who had always been so kind to him.

My mother in France, 1947

STARTING OVER

Elsa was a non-Jewish German woman who, as a young girl, had moved into my grandparents' home in Chemnitz. I never found out why she had no family of her own, but I do know she was like a sister to my mother and they were overjoyed to be reunited.

Elsa had married my father's best friend, a Jewish man named Hershel. Before the war she had wanted to convert to Judaism but the rabbi seemed disingenuous when he offered a special rate for a faster conversion. In the end they had a civil marriage and then they escaped to France in 1933. In 1942, Hershel was deported and sent to a concentration camp. Thankfully the Nazis did not have Elsa in their sights and she remained in Paris throughout the war.

Elsa had a spare room in her apartment at Rue Richer 20 in the 9th *arrondissement* and she took us in. It was a very comfortable arrangement for us, particularly since she lived next door to my grandparents. I slept on a folding cot and each morning before breakfast I would fold everything away in preparation for the day.

Through a Jewish organisation, my mother made contact
with two of my father's cousins who had moved to the United States
before the war. Sam Fuks (later Fox) had become an officer in the US
army and worked as a translator. Sam visited us in Paris several times
over the next few years. When we reached out to the other cousin,
she kindly sent us enough money to purchase a sewing machine.

We were allowed to live in France as refugees but there was
a lot of unemployment and preference was given to French people
seeking work. Luckily, Elsa was a seamstress doing piecework
from home and she was able to take on extra work that she could
delegate to us. One of my grandparents' attics became a dedicated
workroom where my mother and I spent our days cutting garments
and sewing them together to create ladies' fashion items.

After a time, Elsa's boss realised that one outworker could
not possibly be sewing at such a speed and Elsa was forced to
admit that three of us were doing the work. From then on, her boss
– a Jewish lady – gave us the work directly but paid us half the
rate. She also gave us the dregs – smaller parcels and unmatched
fabrics. But it was our bread and butter and we could not refuse,
even when she gave us work that needed to be done on *Yom
Kippur*. We lived in a Jewish area and, while everyone else was
walking to synagogue, I was running around delivering huge bags
of clothing. By then, I had become increasingly conscious of my
Jewish identity and I remember feeling embarrassed and exploited.

I enjoyed learning how to make beautiful clothes from my
mother and we could not complain: at last we had a home, a
family and a source of income. We were also grateful to be living
in one of the most beautiful cities in the world. After so many years
of fear and uncertainty living in the Soviet Union and post-war
Poland, Paris was like paradise and we relished our freedom.

There is a German saying 'the sky is full of violins'. That is how I suddenly felt: surrounded by music, dancing, beauty, culture and, for the first time, friends. My mother's school friend Marta had twin daughters my age, Gita and Irene, and I became particularly friendly with Irene. Their family had been in France since 1932 and were already well established and living in the exclusive 16th *arrondissement*.

Irene and I spent our weekends together and would often go to Jewish community dances, the theatre or the opera with her other friends. I will never forget the wonder of seeing my first play, *Of Mice and Men*. I never had much spending money but I could afford standing room tickets. At the opera we would watch from the top floor and then we would run down to the dress circle to applaud the singers at the end of the performance.

I started learning French at night but the school was far away and, after working all day, I would struggle to keep my eyes open during class. Luckily I had an aptitude for languages and, despite dropping out of the course, I picked up spoken French quickly. I often babysat my little cousins Mira and Susie and they would correct me whenever I made a mistake – they turned out to be great teachers.

Because fabric was still being rationed, my uncle decided to open a factory that made bathing costumes, which did not require too much material. Nathan was not a citizen so he needed a French director on the books. The director took a large percentage of the profits but Nathan still made enough money to support his family and my grandparents. He was also able to support my mother and me by providing us with plenty of work.

My mother (right) with Jenny
and Mira in France, 1947

Me with Susie in France, 1947

ROMANCE

One day, my mother's friend Marta showed me a photo. "This is my nephew, David Hampel," she said. "He's 26 years old and I think you two should meet." I was only 18 but it was not the age difference that concerned me. I said, "Marta, he is not the man for me. He looks like a movie star! He is too handsome and every skirt will be after him." Marta said nothing further, but she secretly invited David to come to Paris.

David and his parents were living in Milan and were preparing to immigrate to Australia. It was 1948 and were in a hurry because they had a permit that had already been extended twice. But of course I did not know any of that at the time. Nor did I know how difficult it was for him to travel to Paris because of his refugee status: David was born in Germany but had Polish citizenship because that is where his parents were born. In order to travel to France, David had to apply for a transit visa that allowed him to take a train through Switzerland.

One night, Irene invited me and some other friends for dinner. David was there and I was one of several young women at the table, including a very tall woman who wore a fur jacket and a slim skirt. David told me afterwards that he had not been shown a photo of me and he had worried that "the ostrich girl" was the one Marta had wanted him to meet.

My first impressions were correct: David was good-looking and charming, flirtatious and somewhat vain. But he also struck me as a man with good values. He travelled on Saturdays but observed *Shabbat* by not smoking, even when everyone around him smoked. I was impressed; he had principles and discipline.

The next day, Gita, Irene, David and I had lunch at a café and spent the afternoon together. Over the next few days we all met as a group and sometimes David's two aunties, Marta and Ida, also came along. I sensed that David liked me, but we had not spent a moment alone together, so it was difficult to know how he was really feeling. Finally, on the fifth day, David invited me to go to the opera with him. We saw *The Tales of Hoffman* – just the two of us – and it was lovely. That is when we kissed for the first time.

The next day we went for a walk along the elegant Champs Élysées before stopping at one of the many sidewalk cafés. We were talking when David suddenly declared, "Ruth, I would like to marry you". Before I could process what was happening he continued, "but before you decide you must know that there are two conditions: first, you must be willing to come with my parents and me to Australia, and second, we must keep a kosher home". The second condition was easy. I did not care about kosher or not kosher; as long as there was food to eat, I was happy. But the first condition perplexed me; I had never even considered marriage, let alone moving to Australia.

I did not tell anybody about the proposal – not Irene, not my mother and not my grandmother. I wanted the decision to be my own, free from any external influence or pressure. The next day I met David and gave him my answer: yes, I would marry him.

My mother was shocked at first but my grandmother was immediately pleased. She was relieved that my mother, who was presumed to be a widow, would not have to worry about me. It was my uncle Nathan who really objected saying, "You hardly know the man. Why would you go to the end of the world with him?" But I had made up my mind and he could see that I was determined. I could be an obstinate young woman.

I introduced David to my family and we set a date for the wedding. I prayed that my grandfather, who was in hospital at the time, would recover and be able to attend. The next morning, before leaving Paris, David rang his parents and I spoke to them in German. They sounded nice but a little bit surprised by our big news. We said our goodbyes and David promised to send me a telegram to let me know he had arrived back in Milan safely.

Unfortunately, I did not receive a telegram. I was very upset, particularly when I found out that David had sent one to Marta. Finally, a letter arrived and my reply was cold. How could he have failed to send me a telegram? How could I trust him? David replied in his next letter: "When I see you I will show you the stamp that proves I sent two telegrams". He described the unreliability of the Italian postal system and soon all was forgiven.

David with his parents, 1923

THE HAMPEL FAMILY

David was born in Frankfurt in 1921. When he was four years old, his mother Ruchla gave birth to a baby boy named Bernard. The family was living in a tiny apartment and there was not even enough room for a cot so, after she stopped breastfeeding, Ruchla make the painful decision to put Bernard in a children's home. She did not feel capable of looking after him and genuinely thought that he would be better off. Tragically, Bernard contracted pneumonia and died at the age of 13 months. Ruchla was overwhelmed by grief and guilt; she never forgave herself for her baby's death and refused to speak his name again.[1]

David's father, Zissman, continued to build up his leather manufacturing business and began exporting leather goods to England and Switzerland. He had learned leather craftsmanship as a young man in Poland in secret, knowing that his Chassidic father would disapprove. The family became established and, when he turned six, David began attending Philanthropin, a well-respected progressive Jewish school founded by Mayer Rothschild.[2]

---

1 In 2000, David and I visited Bernard's grave in Frankfurt but were disturbed to find that there was no headstone. His parents had obviously been so broken that they did not have the emotional strength to arrange one. I later tried to address this injustice by putting a plaque on my husband's grave that memorialised Bernard's birth and death.

2 Philanthropin was a notable Jewish educational institution founded in 1805. At its peak it had 1000 students before being forced to close in 1942. It later reopened and by 2018 had 400 enrolled pupils – two thirds have a Jewish background.

*(Clockwise from above left) David's parents'
engagement in 1920, David in 1923, David in 1924,
David's parents hiding pregnancy*

David at seven

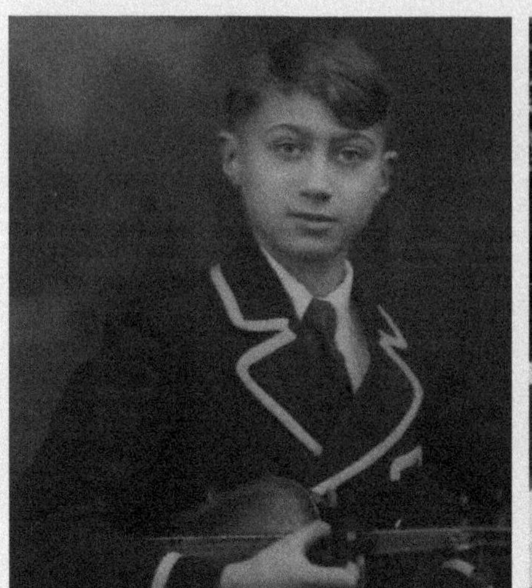

*(Clockwise from above left) Budding violinist David,
David at high school, David's grandfather, c. 1930,
David with his aunt Martha and grandmother*

(Above) David and his parents, 1936
*(Below) David's parents on holidays
in Belgium, 1937*

Hampel was a Germanic surname and the business had a good reputation. So when Hitler imposed a boycott on Jewish businesses, Zissman was fortunate to be allowed to continue trading. For a while, the family's life remained relatively unchanged despite the growing threat of Nazism. However, one morning in 1937, David rode his bike – a gift he had received for his *bar mitzvah* – straight into an SS officer. The officer started yelling at David until an onlooker said, "Leave him alone, he's only a child". Of course, this infuriated the Nazi who threatened to arrest the man. The crowd quickly dispersed and David grabbed his bike and raced home. David's grandmother saw the event from the balcony and decided that it was time to get David out of Germany. The next day, his parents put David on a train bound for Switzerland where he was enrolled in a Jewish boarding school called Institute Asher in Bex-les-Bains.

A few months later, in February 1938, the doorbell rang at the Hampel family home in Frankfurt. David's father answered the door and momentarily lost his ability to speak from the shock of seeing an SS officer standing in the doorway. The man introduced himself saying, "My surname is also Hampel. So I am wondering, are we related?" David's mother Ruchla intervened saying, "I wish we were, but sadly we have no relatives here". Sensing imminent danger, David's grandmother moved quickly. She packed two suitcases and insisted that David's parents also leave for Switzerland immediately. The Hampels were fortunate to both have Polish passports and Swiss visas they had previously acquired for their export business. Also, as a safeguard, they had been sending money into Switzerland via their doctor who had a brother in Zurich. Unfortunately, David's grandmother, a deeply religious woman who wore a *sheitl*, did not have a passport and had no choice but to stay behind and await her fate.

A few months after arriving in Switzerland, David's parents realised that the high cost of living there would drain their savings. They took David out of boarding school and travelled to Milan, figuring they would be safe in northern Italy and that Milan would be a good place to re-establish themselves in the leather industry. However, eight months after arriving in Italy, Mussolini introduced racial laws that prohibited Jews from working and the family decided to return to Switzerland. Unfortunately, David did not have a valid passport and Ruchla's visa to Switzerland had expired. Just as the clerk at the consulate was about to extend the visa, her superior told her the policy had just been changed and they were no longer authorised to make the extension. Zissman pleaded with the authorities but to no avail. They had been seconds too late.

The family decided to attempt to enter Switzerland individually. Dressed as an Italian worker, David managed to cross the border illegally by train to Mendrisio, a small industrial town in the Italian province of Switzerland. Once in Switzerland, David travelled to Lugano where he knew he could stay with a Jewish friend named Belovitz. Next to enter Switzerland was Zissman. Equipped with a passport and a visa, Zissman entered the country with relative ease, bringing with him as many of their possessions as possible. It was Ruchla who had the most challenging time entering Switzerland: she paid someone to smuggle her across the border at night but, on the first attempt, she was caught by Swiss guards and sent back. She tried again the following week and was successful.

For the next two years, David and his parents lived in relative safety in a tiny village called Campione d'Italia in an Italian enclave governed by the Swiss. They boarded in a cottage on a big estate owned by three sisters who had inherited the property from their prosperous parents. Another Jewish family from Frankfurt was also living in a house on the estate. Two of the sisters and their husbands were very nice but unfortunately one of the sisters was married to a member of the fascist party.[3] One day, whilst David was visiting his friends in Lugano, the Nazi sympathiser announced he was under orders from the Italian fascists to escort Zissman back to Italy, along with the father and two teenage sons from the other family. They were taken to an internment camp in Ferramonti di Tarsia in Calabria. David and his mother immediately went into hiding in Lugano. They lived in separate safe houses and, with the help of the local Jewish community, they were continuously moved around. The presence of servants and neighbours made it too dangerous for Jewish non-citizens to stay in one place for too long because the Swiss government was working with the Germans to ensure that Jewish refugees could not remain there permanently. The Swiss had also started building labour camps for refugees and adding a 'J' for Jewish in passports.[4]

Eventually, the authorities discovered that David and his mother were in hiding and interned them in separate labour camps. Although conditions were difficult, the refugee camps were not nearly as brutal or deadly as the Nazi concentration camps in other parts of Europe. David was sent to a dilapidated castle outside Lugano where he was tasked with the job of planting potatoes in springtime and harvesting them in autumn. David told the story of one nasty commandant who made six men carry

---

3 Many years later we visited the estate and met all three sisters. The two kind sisters were very welcoming but the one who had been married to a fascist was clearly uncomfortable and cold towards us.

4 Approximately 100,000 Jewish refugees passed through Switzerland during World War II but only about one third were allowed to stay in the country.

*David planting and harvesting potatoes
in the Swiss detention camp*

a piano up a flight of stairs so they could perform a concert – but that type of cruelty was a far cry from the atrocities being meted out elsewhere.[5] David's mother was interned in a refugee camp located between Zurich and Bern where her assigned task was mending second-hand clothes. The rules at both camps were lax; they were occasionally allowed to leave the camps and, with permission, David would travel by train to meet his mother. They were also able to communicate by letter with David's father in Italy.

Zissman was also treated relatively well in the Italian detention camp. One day he asked one of the nicer commandants if he could rent a room from a widow in the village instead of living in the dormitory with 50 other men. The commandant agreed to his request on the condition that he report to the camp daily. Another Jewish man married a local Italian woman and was also allowed to live outside the camp. Those two men were the lucky ones: a few weeks after Zissman rented the room, the Germans entered the camp, rounded up the refugees and transported them all to Auschwitz. Zissman and the other Jewish man living in the village were the only two who avoided this deadly fate.[6]

By 1944, when it became obvious that the Germans were losing the war, the rules in the Swiss camps changed again to allow refugees to leave if they found employment. David got a job as an apprentice at the Belovitz family's shirt factory and, shortly after, he and his mother were allowed to live together in a small two-room apartment in Lugano.

––––––––––––

5 A few years later in Melbourne my husband spotted a Viennese man called Asher riding a bike. He recognised him as the young man from the camp who recited poetry. We tracked him down and he advised that another mutual acquaintance was coming to Australia with his family. The next day we opened the paper and found a lovely picture of new immigrants Mr and Mrs Fred Adler and their three children. Fred had played the drums at cultural events at the camp. We became friends with these men and their families as well Robert Blau who had been the head waiter in charge of the kitchen at the camp.

6 Only five people from the camp survived the war.

Z. HAMPER   SOUTHEND ON SEA
Whitegate Road 81

L. HAMPER   LONDON
Tower Bridge Road 3 - 5

J. Zlotnicky   LONDON
10, Finsbury Square

Dr. Mitchel LANG   Dental Surgeon   Phone Spe 8046
151 Golders Green Road   LONDON N.W.11

Fritz STARK   C/O Horsfield Sons & Mackrell Bros Ltd.
4 Bunhill Row   LONDON E.C.1
(off Chiswell Street)

COMUNITÀ ISRAELITA
LUGANO

CONTO CHÈQUES POSTALI N. XIa. 123

LUGANO, le 22 mars 1940

ACTE DE BONNES MŒURS

Le Comité de la Communauté Israëlite de Lugano, à la
demande de Mr. David HAMPEL, fils de Zysman HAMPEL,
et de Ruchla née Kokotek, d'origine polonaise, né le 15 décembre 1921, à Francfort sur le Main, :

Déclare que le prénommé D a v i d HAMPEL, qui
est né le 15 décembre 1921, et a demeuré en notre ville de-
puis deux ans env., n'a été l'objet d'aucun rapport ni
d'aucune plainte, qu'il s'est toujours conduit d'une façon
honnête et correcte et que jamais rien de défavorable sur
sa personne n'est venu à notre connaissance.

Donné à Lugano, le 22 mars 1940.

Au Nom de la Communauté:

pr. Le Président en act.   Le Secrétaire

*(Clockwise from above) David's apprenticeship
exam certificate from Lugano, Hampel
leather order, Jewish Community of Lugano
recommendation of good character for David*

*(Clockwise from above) David skiing in Switzerland,
my mother-in-law (left) with her sister-in-law and friend,
David and his parents in Italy, c.1946*

After the war, Zissman was not able to re-enter Switzerland, and
Switzerland wanted refugees to leave the country, so David and his
mother decided to return to Milan. But first the family planned to
make some money buying and selling Swiss watches on the black
market. They chose a meeting spot at the border where Zissman
would throw money tied to a stone over the barbed wire fence.
David and Ruchla would then buy watches and throw them back
over the fence at a designated time.

When the family was finally reunited in Milan, they were
given priority with respect to accommodation because they had
been in Italy before the racial laws had been introduced. They
secured a large apartment with enough space to start their own
shirt-making business. David would cut the fabric as he had been
taught as an apprentice in Lugano, and he would send it to a
machinist to create the garment.

The family was happy enough in post-war Italy but corruption
was endemic; even the police commissioner would buy shirts with
bundles of lire hidden under his coat.

Ruchla's sister, Sala Weisberg had moved to Melbourne with
her husband and four children. They wrote of the opportunities
available in Australia for those prepared to work hard. So David and
his parents began the process of applying to live in Australia. When
the permits were granted, the family decided to extend their time
in Italy in order to save some more money. Later, they successfully
reapplied and were told to arrive in Australia by July 1948 or risk
losing their migrant status.

*My paternal grandfather on
holiday in Les Sables-d'Olonne*

LOSS

My grandfather died in May 1948, a week after Israel was declared an independent state and a month before my wedding. He was 70 years old.

My grandfather and I had only known each other for two years, but we had tried to make up for lost time and had developed a pleasant relationship. We even went on a holiday together to a seaside town in western France called Les Sables-d'Olonne. I will never forget the smile on his face when I presented him with a single flower on his 70th birthday, as was the custom in those days.

We buried my grandfather in the Jewish cemetery in Paris and a rabbi gave the eulogy. Then there was a collection for the Jewish National Fund in Israel. My mother was stoic but it was the first funeral I had ever attended and I became hysterical. So much pent-up grief came gushing out of me. I had lost my father, I had lost my uncle Sam and there was no one left in Poland. It all burst out of me. I was totally inconsolable.

Our wedding day, 1948

A WEDDING

David and his parents arrived in Paris on 1 June 1948 and moved into a small hotel while we started the complicated process of getting married. The first step was to arrange a civil wedding and then we could have a religious ceremony.

My first impressions of my future parents-in-law were positive. Ruchla struck me as a warm person who was easy to get along with. She was the type of woman who would say what was on her mind and then immediately move on and have a cup of tea. Zissman was a quiet man who hated confrontation and who liked things to be in order, which is why he hated the corruption that was so prevalent in Milan. He also hated the way the Italians hung their washing across the street. Zissman had two favourite sayings that always made me laugh: "Water is to wash the dishes" and "Salad is good for the goats".

In France at the time, you had to put your names on a list outside the town hall for a month and, if nobody objected during that period, you were then allowed to marry. But, because David had not been living in Paris, we needed special dispensation from a senior judge to have a civil marriage. The process was further complicated by the fact that I was not a French citizen; I was a mere refugee who had to report annually to the police to be fingerprinted.

It took us several weeks of filling in forms, having medical tests and meeting with bureaucrats before we were finally able to appear before the judge. Our hearts dropped when the judge's secretary said it would take several weeks to grant the dispensation. My fiancé asked if there was anything we could do to speed up the process and the secretary said yes, there were ways and means. So, David discreetly paid a bribe and we were told to come back the next day to collect the signed form. The corruption made me furious; I had hoped that things would be different after I left the Soviet Union.

On Tuesday 6 July, David and I married at a civil service at the Hotel de Ville. I wore a lovely navy dress that my mother had made with material she purchased with saved coupons. It had a cinched waist and was quite long, a style that was just becoming fashionable. My mother, my grandmother, Jenny and Nathan, and David's parents were all present to witness our marriage.

Five days later, on Sunday 11 July, we were married by a rabbi under a *chuppah* at my aunt and uncle's home. We were surrounded by family including Irene, Gita and Marta. During the ceremony my uncle Nathan said, "If anybody knows a presentable man for my sister-in-law (referring to my mother), I have a spare *ketubah*".[1] I remember being terribly upset that he had been so inappropriate at such a solemn moment. He was obliquely referring to the fact that, after the war, the rabbinate declared that if someone had been missing for seven years, they were presumed dead and their spouse could remarry *halachically*. I angrily told my uncle afterwards that everything would happen for my mother in good time.[2]

---

1 Jewish marriage contract.

2 I was proven right five years later when my mother married Maurice Klipper who was a wonderful man!

Our civil ceremony, 1948

Our civil ceremony, 1948

N° 1661. *Mariage Hampel* 365 *2 fois*
754

IIe Lot. — N° 15.011

PRÉFECTURE DE LA SEINE

EXTRAIT des Minutes des Actes de Mariage

Mairie

du 9e Arrondissement

B/

Coût de cette expédition : 15 francs

1948

A N° 027433

le six juillet mil neuf cent quarante-huit, onze heures, acte
de mariage de : Dawid Isak HAMPEL, né à Francfort sur le Mein
(Allemagne), le quinze décembre mil neuf cent vingt-un, domici-
lié à Paris, 16 Avenue de Tourville ; fils de Sisman dit Sali
HAMPEL, et de Ruehla KOKOTEK, son épouse, d'une part./.- et de:
Ruth FUKS, née à Varsovie (Pologne) le neuf janvier mil neuf
cent trente, domiciliée à Paris, 20 rue Richer * fille de Max
FUKS et de Stella MUSZKATBLAT, son épouse, d'autre part./.-
Sans contrat de mariage.- les futurs ont déclaré, l'un après
l'autre, vouloir se prendre pour époux, et Nous, Jean Marcel
GLAIZE, Adjoint au maire du IXe Arrondissement de Paris, avons
prononcé, au nom de la Loi, qu'ils sont unis par le mariage./

PPUR EXTRAIT CONFORME,

PARIS, le huit juillet mil neuf cent quarante-huit.

LE MAIRE,

*Celebrations following our religious
wedding ceremony, 1948*

The apartment was filled with fragrant flowers, which had been given to us as wedding gifts because, in those days, giving money was seen as charity. My uncle and aunt arranged a delicious feast and I contributed by baking several sponge cakes. It was a quiet party with no music because we were still mourning my grandfather's recent death. Nevertheless, everyone was in a good mood and pleased to see us so obviously in love and happily wed.

———————————

My Australian travel document photograph

LIMBO

The next administrative hoop we had to jump was to arrange my visa to Australia. The plan was that I would secure my permit in time to travel to Australia with my husband. There was no Australian embassy in Paris so we were arranging everything through the British Embassy. A Jewish agency was also assisting us.

I finally received my permit the day David was due to depart Paris by plane. But then I was told that I still needed a medical certificate. I said a tearful goodbye to David and promised to be on the plane scheduled to leave two weeks later; my father-in-law had booked me a seat assuming that I would be allowed to depart.

With my x-rays and blood test results in hand, I went to see the doctor at the British Embassy who said I needed a full examination. He proceeded to put his hand right under my skirt before I slapped him. Hard. He grabbed my x-rays and said he could not give me a certificate because I had tuberculosis. I knew he was lying because the x-rays had been examined only a few weeks earlier before the wedding. I had no choice but to leave the embassy and make an appointment to see another doctor who specialised in pulmonary diseases. He looked at my x-ray and said, "All I see here are fingerprints. Go and have another x-ray". I took the new x-ray back to the British Embassy praying that the same doctor would not be on duty. Thankfully, he was not. I secured the medical certificate I needed, but of course, by then, my plane was long gone. The whole exercise had taken two months.

I was told a boat to Australia was soon leaving from Marseille. So, after tearfully farewelling my family, I travelled to Marseille and tried to secure a ticket, along with a large contingent of Jewish migrants keen to leave Europe. I soon discovered there was a strike at the docks and that the ship's departure was indefinitely delayed. I rang my family to share the news. They urged me to return to Paris immediately, claiming it was unsafe for me to remain in Marseille on my own. Unwilling to turn back, I ignored their advice. I found a cheap hotel and decided to wait for the strike to end. After almost a month of waiting, I reluctantly agreed to return to my family.

When I arrived in Paris, I discovered that my uncle had sent David a telegram stating: "Ruth has returned to Paris". I was furious at the brevity of the message and realised that David would assume I had changed my mind about going to Australia. To make matters worse, it was virtually impossible for David to book a phone call to Europe. King George had been due to travel to Australia so the press had reserved all the incoming and outgoing international calls. The king's trip was eventually cancelled due to illness, so finally, after several weeks of trying, David scheduled a call to my aunt's apartment. I had been staying there for fear of

My grandmother and I farewell
David as he departs for Australia

missing his call. The first thing he asked was, "Darling, do you still love me?" I quickly responded, "Of course I do!" I told him what had happened in Marseille and, hearing the tears in my voice, he immediately said he would send me 500 pounds – a fortune in those days – to ensure I had enough money to travel to Australia by plane. The call took place in my aunt's lounge room with everyone present, including my grandmother, mother, aunt and David's two aunts. I was embarrassed and upset not to have any privacy.

I went to see a man called Mr Susskind who, I had been told, could purchase a ticket on my behalf. He booked me a flight due to depart on 31 December 1948 and everyone was excited that I would be celebrating the new year as I moved through each time zone. When that plane was cancelled, I became desperate. Each day in limbo felt like a lifetime.

On 17 January 1949, after so many frustrating months of waiting and countless false starts, I finally bid farewell to my family for the last time and left Paris. Having been so recently reunited with her family, my mother did not feel ready to leave Paris but she promised to join me in Australia in the not-too-distant future. After years of living together and relying solely on each other for survival, travelling without my mother was a peculiar but liberating experience. I was strangely calm as I embarked on the journey to my new life. I felt free.

I'M HERE

The voyage to Australia was an adventure in itself. I left Paris
in a small plane with 11 other passengers. We landed in
Brussels and waited in the airport overnight for another flight
to Athens. From Athens we flew to Delhi, from Delhi to Mumbai
and then on to Singapore. In Singapore I was shocked to learn
that I needed a visa; an authority in Paris had told me a visa was
not needed because I would remain in transit. The Singaporean
airport authorities then confiscated my 'stateless travel document'
and escorted me to a hotel in a Chinese area. I was effectively
placed under house arrest. I was then interrogated about whether
I was a communist; the policemen kept pointing to a red star to
convey their message. Of course I could not respond properly
because I did not speak English and no attempt was made to
arrange a translator. I did my best to communicate by referring to
the big French–English dictionary I had brought with me.

For a whole day, a night and a second day, I was kept in that
room with intermittent visits from the police for more useless

questioning. The situation was not unfamiliar to me given my experience growing up in the Soviet Union. But I also knew that the fact I had done nothing wrong was not a guarantee that justice would prevail. I tried my best to remain calm throughout the chilling ordeal, comforting myself with thoughts of a happy reunion with my husband.

Finally, it became clear that I would be allowed to leave on my 2am flight. Someone came to the hotel room, handed me back my travel document and escorted me into a taxi. When the taxi driver tried to drop me off in front of a British army garrison in the middle of the night, I started yelling in French, "No! Airport!" I put my hand over the boot to stop the driver removing my suitcase from the car. The commotion caused an army officer to come over and redirect the taxi driver to the airport. I did not breathe until I saw the lights of the runway.

Finally, I found myself sitting on a luxurious British Airways flight to Sydney. The relief was overwhelming. The aircraft was all one class and it felt like I was in a fancy restaurant when I was greeted by a friendly steward dressed in white. I was seated next to a charming young lady from Sydney who invited me to meet her family and have a short tour of the city while waiting for my next flight. She even drove me back to the airport when it was time for me to embark on the final leg of my journey.

At the airport, I rang the number David had given me to reach his friend who had a telephone and a car. I told him what time my flight was scheduled to arrive. Then a flight attendant told me that I could take an earlier flight. After all the delays, I could not resist the opportunity to get to my final destination sooner, so I ran to catch the flight. I landed in Melbourne, navigated my way through immigration and customs, and searched for the taxi queue.

The taxi driver asked if I minded sharing the ride with another passenger travelling to the Prince of Wales Hotel in St Kilda. As we drove along the beach, I marvelled at the glorious blue skies and the palm trees lining the esplanade. I arrived at my in-law's house in Mayfield Road just as everyone was getting into the car, including my mother-in-law who was carrying an enormous bouquet of flowers. I yelled out, "I'm here. I'm here!"

At the age of 19, I was finally home. It was a lovely new beginning for me.

GRAVES & COULSON

PART TWO

AUSTRALIA

1949–2006

With David in 1954

HOMECOMING

It had been six months to the day since I had last seen my husband and, over the course of our short marriage, we had only spent 11 days together. I stared at David in wonder; everything in my life until that point had felt so transitory that it was difficult to truly accept that we would never need to be apart again. It was an indescribable feeling.

David filled me in on what had happened since we had parted. Upon arriving in Australia, David and his parents moved into a rooming house in Rathdowne Street, Carlton arranged by Ruchla's sister Sala and her husband Wolfe Weisberg. At the time, Carlton was the centre of Jewish life in Melbourne and to David and his cosmopolitan parents it felt like a *shtetl*. They hated it and dismissively referred to the wrought iron balconies on the Victorian terrace houses as 'iron curtains'. Within days, they started to explore other parts of Melbourne and found the south-eastern suburb of St Kilda more appealing. While out one day looking for a place to live in St Kilda, the family's belongings were stolen in a robbery; the thieves had broken into their room and taken silk shirts, handmade shoes and other items of value. It was an unfortunate beginning.

Thanks to his boarding school education in Switzerland, David spoke perfect English and was able to negotiate the 400 pounds needed for key money and the rent on an upstairs apartment at 8 Mayfield Street, East St Kilda. A man named lived downstairs with his son, daughter-in-law and grandchild. The apartment had a bathroom but the toilet was in an outhouse in the backyard. The accommodation was basic compared to the comfort of the Hampels' homes in Milan and Frankfurt but they were happy to be out of Carlton. The family joined the Caulfield Hebrew Congregation, which was in a house in Inkerman Street and began to settle into their new surroundings.

The Weisbergs were annoyed that the family moved away. Wolfe said, "You moved somewhere with *grosse fenster* (big windows)," implying that David and his parents were looking down on the community. In turn, my in-laws were disappointed by the apparent lack of warmth from their family. My mother-in-law was shocked that their first meal at her sister's home was served in the kitchen and not in the dining room.

To his credit, Wolfe had gone to the effort of leasing premises on the first floor of the arcade at 282 Chapel Street[1] for the family to establish a business in Prahran. However, David decided that he would first do a short stint at the Weimar shirt factory so that he could find out more about how the local fashion industry operated. After two weeks, David decided he had learned enough to devote himself to the task of running his own shirt manufacturing operation and he began buying the necessary equipment and hiring skilled machinists. Very quickly David realised the power of

---

1 The building is currently a JB Hi-Fi store.

the unions and the fact that his business would have to be a closed shop whereby he could only hire union members.

Material was still heavily rationed and could only be purchased through a coupon system. David applied for a licence to import fabric but, as a new immigrant, he had limited status and had to wait patiently for the application to be processed. Meanwhile, Wolfe introduced David to his friend Isaac Czerny and his partner Mr Dorevich. The two men ran a successful wholesaling business and they were extremely generous with their advice and contacts. Isaac introduced David to the buyer at the Ball & Welch emporium in Flinders Street[1] and David impressed him with samples of the silk shirts he had produced in Milan. In reality, the fabric of those shirts had been purchased in Como from a factory that produced parachutes for the Allies. David's samples were beautifully boxed with a butterfly clip holding the shirt in shape. The buyer immediately placed an order but he wanted the shirts unboxed so that they could be stacked flat and more shirts could be stocked on each shelf. Ball & Welch supplied David with the fabric needed to fill each order. The shirts sold well and, before long, orders started flowing in from other up-market stores. Within months, David and his father had 20 employees.

---

2 The historic site of Ball & Welch later became the up-market department store Georges.

FIRST IMPRESSIONS

My mother-in-law invited the Weisbergs and some new friends to an afternoon tea to celebrate my arrival. Jet-lagged, I was still in my dressing gown when Wolfe arrived early. He took one look at me and said, "Ruth, you can't walk around like that. In Australia, only whores paint their toes". Outraged, I said, "Well, that's not the case in Paris!" I wondered what he knew about prostitutes' toes.

A few days later I saw some women dressed up in evening gowns with cigarettes walking down the street by themselves. Only ladies of the night smoked in the streets of Paris, so I asked David if all those aging women were prostitutes. He laughed and said they were just ladies on their way to the local cinema. The way Australians dressed was unsophisticated compared to the French but they still wore gloves, as women did in Paris. It was the men who seemed to be dressed in uniform. Inwardly I laughed at the funny bags they carried to work; in Europe we had called them 'midwives' bags'.

Australia Day was celebrated a week after my arrival. It was a beautiful summer's day and David suggested we go to St Kilda

Beach by tram. After a few wonderful, carefree hours in the sun we took the tram home, all the while chatting happily to each other in French. Suddenly, a fellow wearing a cap and braces tapped David on the shoulder and said, "Why can't you bloody well speak English?" David replied, "It's a private conversation so it's none of your business what language we speak". I remember feeling so proud of David at that moment; he spoke English so beautifully and addressed the man with such polite authority. I had not experienced that kind of loving protection since my father was taken away when I was only seven.

The first time we went to see a film together was at the Palais Theatre in St Kilda. We purchased the tickets a week in advance and saw two features with a newsreel first. After watching the films we had to stand and sing *God Save the King*. Soon we also started frequenting the Victory Theatre on Barkly Street.[1] Of course I was yet to learn English but I still managed to enjoy myself.

English was to be my fifth language. At 19, I had already mastered German, Russian, Polish and French. I had not made any friends yet and had only the dog from downstairs for company, so I listened to the radio all day and tried my best to understand what was being said. I was homesick for my social life in Paris but I knew that it was only a matter of time and patience. I reminded myself that I had travelled to a land of sheep and oranges, and a lot of sunshine. Despite some loneliness, I never doubted that I would have a happy future in Australia.

---

1 Now the National Theatre.

OUR FIRST FACTORY

David had hoped that I would be happy to stay at home with his mother and look after the house. That was not the case. I was slowly making friends but I was going crazy at home with only mundane domestic tasks like shopping, cooking and washing to fill my day. I managed to convince my husband that I would be an asset to the business and I began work on the factory floor folding and pressing shirts. Zissman was also working in the business; he managed the workers while David dealt with the customers. The employees all referred to Zissman as 'Mr Hampel' and David as simply 'David'.

David reinvested all his profits back into the business. At first the factory took up two rooms at each end of the corridor on the right-hand side of the arcade but, within weeks of my arrival, he rented the rooms in between so that the factory took up half the floor. The fact that the factory was upstairs in a building without a lift made access challenging but at least the proximity to Prahran Station allowed all the goods to be couriered to the city stores by train.

Finally, a year after lodging the application, David was granted a licence with a quota to import fabric from England.

There were a lot of mills in England and the prices were competitive. They had only a limited colour range of white, beige and blue but that was all anyone in Australia was wearing. Fashion innovation came later, in the 1960s, when there were less import restrictions and we could buy fabric from anywhere in the world, including Japan where the mills produced fabrics in a glorious range of colours.

Within a year, I was expecting our first baby. I continued to work until I was eight months pregnant when David begged me to stay home, fearing that his employees would mistake him for a slave driver.

With Max, 1951

MOTHERHOOD

To everyone's delight, our first son was born on 23 April 1950. We named him Maxwell (Max) after my beloved father. I had hoped to return to work soon after the birth, but of course I had underestimated how hard it was to look after a newborn baby. I was pleased to at least receive the new child endowment payment of five shillings a week so that I felt like I was still contributing to our family income.

That year, we rented our own home in McHenry Street, which ran parallel to Mayfield Street. I felt extremely proud that we were able to live in our own home so soon after arriving in a new country. Everywhere I had ever lived was a shared and temporary space; this was the first home I could really call my own. I relished the opportunity to furnish the house to my own taste and to live without compromise or fear of judgment from others. I was growing roots.

I wrote often to my mother and shared details about Max's growth and our daily routine. I was thrilled to receive a letter from

her one day in which she wrote that she had met a charming man by
the name of Maurice Klipper. She wrote that they were both keen to
one day move to Australia.

Our second son, Daniel (Danny), was born on 4 January 1952
and Alexander (Alex) came along one year later on 20 February
1953. Having three sons under the age of three was challenging,
so David insisted that I have extra help around the home. We had a
large garden and, as they grew older, the boys loved to play in the
street with other kids from the neighbourhood. They also enjoyed
climbing the back fence to visit their doting grandparents. My father-
in-law was particularly attached to Daniel who I believe reminded
him of the baby boy they had lost many years earlier.

By 1955, we had finally saved enough money to purchase a
home in Glen Eira Road, Elsternwick. Max went to Caulfield Primary
School and Daniel started kindergarten next door at the home of
Mrs Heartz. I found myself home alone with Alex who was suddenly
miserable without his brothers and the friends from McHenry Street
to play with. Mrs Heartz asked me why she could hear Alex crying
so much. I explained that he missed his brothers and she suggested
that he also attend kindergarten; she did not mind that he was
so young, only that he was out of nappies. Alex was pleased and
suddenly it was me who became the unhappy one. I found myself
crying as I made the boys' beds upstairs in the mornings; I could
hear them playing and watch them in the playground through the
window and it made me miserable. My mother-in-law tried to cheer
me up by taking me dress shopping but that did not diminish my
loneliness. I realised that it was time to go back to work. We only
had one car at the time, so I took public transport to the factory in
Chapel Street and I worked each school day from 9.30am till 2pm.

(Clockwise, from top left) David, Ruth, and Max, with Max age three months, my parents-in-law with Max, Alex and Danny in 1954

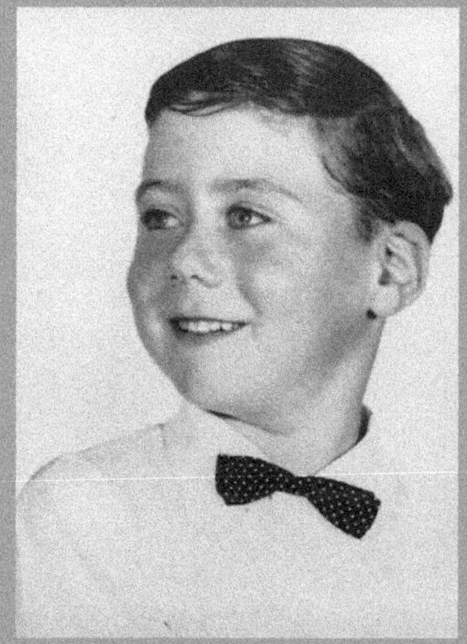
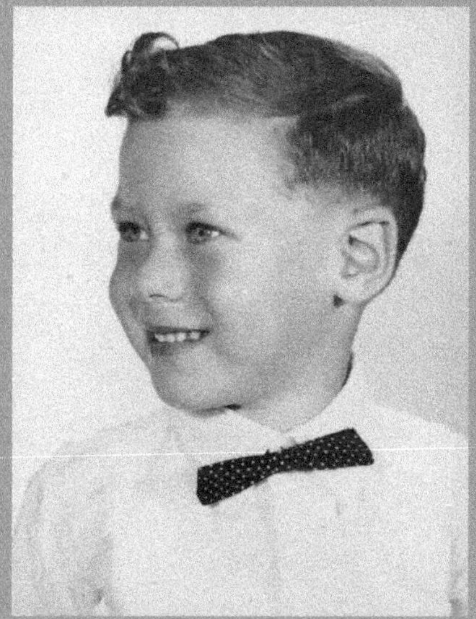

(Clockwise from above left) Max, Danny, Alex, 1956

*(Above) The boys play in the backyard
of our McHenry Street home, 1954
(Below) Our new home in Glen Eira Road, 1955*

With David in Mt Eliza, 1956

(Above) The family in Paris, 1954
(Back) Nathan, Jenny, Maurice, my mother, Maurice's
son Harry, Nathan's sister and her husband
(Front) Mira, my grandmother and Nathan's niece Lillian
(Below) The family in Melbourne, c.1966

My mother and Maurice married in Paris in 1953. My father had officially been presumed dead for many years and, by then, Mum was 48 years old. She wrote that Maurice was a lovely man who was very attentive to her every need; they lived well and she no longer needed to work because Maurice had a wealthy brother who provided financial support. I was pleased that, after so many years of thankless labour, my mother could finally have some time for herself. I was also pleased that she would now become a French citizen. Mostly I was thankful that she was happily settled with a man who would give her love and take good care of her.

I wished I could have been at the wedding and that I could introduce my mother, grandmother, aunt, uncle, and cousins to my sons, but the cost of overseas travel was totally prohibitive so I had to celebrate from a distance. When I left Paris in 1949, I had been certain I would return soon and see everyone in my family again. It was not to be. My much-loved grandmother died in 1958 and I mourned her passing on my own.

Soon after my grandmother's death, Maurice sent me a letter confirming that he and my mother wished to move to Australia. He then outlined all the matters they wanted us to arrange on their behalf, including buying them an apartment and finding him work. It felt like a letter of demand and we could not meet his expectations; after all, we were saving for the expense of educating our three young children at Mount Scopus College and we had a large mortgage. I wrote back that they would not be able to rely on us financially. I confirmed my desire for them to move to Australia but I stressed that if they came to our new country, they would have to support themselves. That was the last I heard from them about moving to Australia.

A NEW FACTORY

Whenever a delivery of material arrived, the factory workers, who were almost all women, would have to haul the rolls of fabric from the truck up the stairwell. The building was not suited to factory work and it was becoming a safety issue. By 1960, it became clear that we had to move to new premises.

David purchased a block of land at 7 Duke Street in nearby Windsor and we all enjoyed planning the design of a purpose-built factory. My mother-in-law was terrible with names but she managed to build a good rapport with all the factory workers by speaking what I called 'Mum's Esperanto' – a mix of Yiddish, German, Polish, Italian and a few words of English. She insisted that we create a well-appointed tearoom with mosaic tiles for the staff members to enjoy their breaks. My father-in-law insisted on wooden floorboards, which would be softer on the workers' feet than concrete, and the union reps demanded we provide a dedicated sick bay. Together we created a fantastic building that we were immensely proud of. Soon the ground floor bustled with the activity of machinists at work, while master cutters created the patterns for our stylish shirts on the top floor.

The union reps would regularly drop in to the factory unannounced, call a stop work and then hold a meeting for an hour. Often they would incite the workers to make unreasonable demands. We had one factory worker from Yugoslavia who, having recently escaped communism, refused to join the union. I was supervising dispatch so I could overhear the reps hassling her to join by promising her higher wages and better conditions. Over time, the reps began to ignore the woman and I suspected that my husband had begun paying her union membership fee. My husband liked to keep the peace and to ensure that his workers were happy. On occasion that extended to him loaning large sums of money to staff members so they could each pay a deposit on a house.

The Eterna Shirt Company continued to grow from strength to strength. Our European-style shirts were manufactured to the highest standards and stylishly presented in boxes with the collar and cuffs on show. Altogether we had 40 employees and we also engaged outworkers when required. David would travel to every state in Australia at least three times a year to present the range to our agents, who would then go on the road selling to retail stores across each state. One of our storemen took over my role managing the dispatch while I enjoyed sorting and packing the orders. My father-in-law continued to manage production until he retired in 1955.

Our first overseas trip, 1967

REUNITED

enjoyed my sons' teenage years. Our beautiful home had a huge garden that was often full of the children that Max, Danny and Alex had befriended from around the neighbourhood.

Life was never dull; at the time there were no traffic lights on the corner of Glen Eira Road and there were often car accidents at the intersection. Our boys would delight in being the first to ring a towing company in order to receive a $5 kickback and I would accuse them of behaving like vultures!

We holidayed as a family in Mount Buffalo and on two occasions we took our sons to the Gold Coast.

In 1961, I was thrilled when my mother accepted our offer to bring her to Melbourne to meet our family. Her husband Maurice decided to stay behind in Paris.

It had been 12 years since I had seen my mother and so much had changed in that time – we were both married women and I was the mother of three young boys – and yet, some things were still exactly the same. From the moment she arrived, I sensed my mother's unhappiness and dissatisfaction. She spoke reasonable English but felt dependent on me to take her everywhere. I immediately fell into my old pattern of feeling responsible for her and simultaneously guilty that I could not adequately fulfil her needs. She craved my attention and I felt suffocated. Our long period of separation had done little to repair the rift between us. The plan had been that my mother would stay with us for six months but, after three months, she decided to return to Paris.

I did not see my mother again until 1967 when David and I returned to Europe for the first time. I had been anxious at the idea of staying with my mother and hoped that we would instead stay in a hotel, but David could not understand my logic and was insistent that we stay with them. I finally met Maurice and, over the next few weeks, I observed that he was indeed totally devoted to my mother. I sensed, however, that her behaviour was slightly erratic and I could also see that Maurice would often cover for her and pretend that everything was fine.

Maurice's son Harry was also living with them. Harry was a pleasant, hard-working young man in his early 20s. He was clearly fond of my mother but I was sometimes embarrassed by the way he was treated. I noted he would come home tired and dirty after a day of working as a lift engineer and Maurice would immediately pass him a bag of rubbish to take back down three flights of stairs. They were always yelling at him to get off the phone and I also found it strange that one of their kitchen cupboards was locked to ensure Harry did not drink their alcohol or eat their good chocolates. Their behaviour reinforced to me that David and I had a very different approach to parenting and a much warmer way of expressing love for our children.

It saddened me that my mother had never really known how to be maternal.

It was lovely to see Jenny, Nathan and my cousins Mira and Susie again. Most exciting of all was that my cousin Sonia travelled from Berlin to see us. Unbelievably, it was the first time I had seen Sonia since our teary separation in Kazakhstan all those years ago. We wept as we reminisced about our childhood as 'second sisters' in Moscow. Even though she was five years older than me, and had been more deeply indoctrinated by communism, Sonia remembered very little about that period. I was shocked when she asked me if I knew why her father had been out of work. I told her the story of how he had needed a doctor's certificate to prevent him being denounced by a jealous workmate. I also shared my deeply held secret about my encounters with the secret police. It was the first time I had ever told anyone about what happened to me as a child – not even my husband knew about the trauma I had experienced.

In Moscow, Sonia had finished her medical degree and had become a professor in biology. She was married to a professor of urology named Moritz. Together they had one daughter named Anna. In 1949, when she was only 24, Sonia lost her beautiful mother Rosa. Realising that there was no reason to remain in Moscow, in 1951, the family moved to East Berlin. Max moved with them and lived independently in his own apartment filled with the wonderful library of books he had managed to keep. My mother and grandmother had the chance to visit them in Berlin before Max died in 1956. Apparently, no one had the heart to tell my grandmother about his passing.

Somehow, the fear of connecting with the regime had prevented me from ever communicating with my family.

*(Above) Reunion with Sonia
(centre of back row) in 1967
(Below) Paris, 1967*

I was upset and ashamed when Sonia told me that Max had always been saddened that I never reached out to him. After the kindness Max and Rosa extended to me, that shame follows me to this day.

After Europe, David and I were excited to travel to Israel for the first time. A chauffeur-driven limousine met us on the tarmac and escorted us to the Dan Hotel in Tel Aviv, which was founded and owned by David's mother's cousin Yekutiel Federman. The Federman family owned a total of eight hotels in Israel at the time and they went to every effort to ensure that we were treated like royalty. We were even lucky enough to meet the legendary Abba Eban who was the minister for foreign affairs.

(Clockwise from above left) Max's bar mitzvah,
Danny's bar mitzvah, *Alex's* bar mitzvah,
The boys at Alex's bar mitzvah

The family at Danny's bar mitzvah

Holidays in Mount Buffalo

Surfers Paradise, 1963

*With Sally and Otto Lorry on Max and
Elizabeth's wedding day, 1972*

TOWARDS UNDERSTANDING

The next time I saw my mother was when she returned to Australia in 1972 to celebrate the wedding of my oldest son Max to Elizabeth (Lizzie) Lorry. Unfortunately, Maurice was already suffering from stomach cancer and was too unwell to travel. At the wedding we missed my much-loved father-in-law who had died whilst on holiday in Surfers Paradise in 1969.

I was pleased that my mother had made the effort to come on her own and she seemed to be in relatively good spirits. I enjoyed watching my sons gallantly attempting to look after her and to bond with the grandmother they hardly knew.

Unfortunately my mother was not able to attend the joyful weddings of our other sons. Danny married Lili Heifetz in 1976. We were then delighted to celebrate Alex's marriage to Suzanne (Sue) Zelig the following year.

When Maurice passed away in 1977, I wrote to my grieving mother and asked her to consider locking up her apartment and moving to Australia on a trial basis. In Paris my mother only had one friend left and my aunt Jenny, who was elderly herself and lived almost an hour away by metro. Jenny reported that Mum occasionally refused to answer the door or the telephone.

In 1978, my mother did as I had suggested: she packed up her belongings and flew to Melbourne. I picked her up from the airport and brought her home to live with us. Over the years, two of my mother's friends had moved to Melbourne and occasionally she made the effort to see them. But often I would come home from work to find my mother sitting in the same spot I had left her eight hours earlier. Alzheimer's was not well understood at that time but it was obvious to me that my mother's mental state was deteriorating. We arranged for her to move into an apartment in an independent living complex with on-site medical services. A lot of German-speaking people lived in the complex so she was able to form friendships with the other residents.

My aunt Jenny came to Australia for the first time in 1981. By then, we had rebuilt our house. I offered for her to stay with us but she declined, saying she had come to see her sister and would stay with her. After a few days she regretted the decision and reported that Mum was acting weirdly and looking at her as though she had come to steal her belongings.

My mother never went back to Paris. She passed away in 1988 at the age of 84. One year later, my mother-in-law also died, having outlived her husband by 20 years.

In her strange way, my mother had loved me but it had never felt like the warm, protective force that had emanated from my father. The persecution she suffered, the torture, fear, dislocation and other hardships had damaged her soul. With no access to counselling or understanding of post-traumatic stress, those issues had never been addressed; instead I had carried the burden of caring for her as a young girl despite suffering from my own personal trauma.

Reading *The Whisperers*[1] 10 years ago was a revelation for me and signalled the end of the long and emotional journey I had to endure before I could finally begin to understand my mother. The overwhelming flood of detail that emerged in this brilliant and devastating book conveys the psychological pain inflicted by Stalinism. As one reviewer stated, "The camps killed millions but also wasted the inner lives of millions more". My mother's experiences during those terrible years left her unable to express emotion or affection – in truth, she had nothing left of herself to give to me.

____

1 *The Whisperers – Private Life in Stalin's Russia* by Orlando Figes, 2007.

My mother-in-law and mother, 1978

Danny and Lili's wedding day, 1976

Alex and Sue's wedding day, 1977

A NEW ERA

Eventually the boys all finished school and their various tertiary studies and began working in the business. At one point all three boys were working with us! It was gratifying to have built a business that was big enough to offer interesting opportunities for our sons to learn and grow professionally.

After several years, Max and Daniel both branched out on their own. Watching them pursue their dreams filled us with pride. Alex had always intended to follow in his father's footsteps and he worked together with us as the business transformed from manufacturing into wholesale. Together we opened menswear stores in Toorak and Brighton in the late '70s.

In 1973, Whitlam's government cut tariffs by 25 per cent, opening the floodgates to imports. It became increasingly difficult to manufacture locally and remain competitive so we closed our factory. We had to let our workers go, which was heartbreaking. Thankfully a government initiative ensured they received a substantial payout, which made the decision easier to bear.

As the decade came to a close, a decision was made to sell the import quota and close the wholesale company. Alex wanted to grow the retail business and David, who only lasted six months in retirement, joined the fledgling venture. This period was exciting for me as I was able to continue being involved in the business until 1994 when I felt ready to retire and devote more time to family.

By then, David and I had become grandparents to seven wonderful children: Max and Lizzie's sons Avraham and Ronnie; Danny and Lili's children Natalie and Jonathan; and Alex and Sue's sons Rodney, Bradley and Dean. We loved spending time with each grandchild one-on-one and sharing *Shabbat* dinner with our growing extended family.

With our seven grandchildren, 2001

With David in Cairns, 1996

MY SAVIOUR

My husband passed away in 2006, five days after his 85th birthday. I was comforted by the fact that he was able to live at home until the end. Several years earlier we had designed a purpose-built home at 11 Palm Avenue that allowed him to live in comfort despite ongoing heart problems and back pain. David had particularly loved our swimming pool, which he cleaned fastidiously every day.

My husband was raised with old-fashioned values. He was a cherished son, particularly after the death of his baby brother, and some would argue that he was spoiled and patriarchal, but I did not see him that way. Alex once said in frustration, "In our household, Dad is the king". I remember replying, "Yes. And I am the queen!"

To me, David was a wonderful husband, gentleman and scholar. It is true that he could be rather stern and controlling at times but if ever I disagreed with him, he would listen to my views and respect my opinions. I vividly recall that on one occasion,

David gave a large donation to United Israel Appeal and I was upset to see that on the pledge form he had written "David Hampel". After the event I said to him, "Am I not your partner in life and in business?" Straight away he saw the error in his ways and it never happened again.

David had studied the Talmud from an early age and remained religious throughout his life. He was a committed member of St Kilda Synagogue and he served as treasurer, and then president of the congregation for three years. In 2005, he was inducted as a life governor, an honour bestowed on a person of learning and integrity. David personally tutored each of his grandsons for their *bar mitzvahs* and he beamed with pride as they read from the Torah as he stood beside them on the *bimah*. My proudest moment was when, in 2006, all 10 Hampel men sang together on the bimah to celebrate the 72nd anniversary of David's *bar mitzvah*.

After being raised without any knowledge of Judaism, I adapted to David's religious ways and enjoyed attending synagogue and keeping a kosher home. When you eat cooked grass as a child, you appreciate that food is food! David introduced me to the joys of *Shabbat* and I treasured our Friday night meals at home, shared with family and friends.

Looking back, I see clearly that my husband was my saviour. He taught me how to love and how to be loved, and he brought me to a country where I felt safe and protected. Together we built a business and raised a wonderful family. I am forever grateful.

———————

With my husband, 1976

(Clockwise from above left) Lugano in 1973, Manila in 1974, with David in Manila, Hawaii in 1992, Norway

Alaska, 1988

On a cruise with David

(Clockwise from above left) Fiji, Brussels, Uluru, Surfers Paradise

(Above) Our 50th wedding anniversary
(Below) David's 85th birthday

(Clockwise from above) David in his study at our Glen Eira Road home, Hawaii, Surfers Paradise in 2005

EPILOGUE

As someone who grew up as an only child, I often marvel at the size of our growing family. I have been blessed with three incredible sons, seven wonderful grandchildren and 11 great-grand-children, all of whom make me enormously proud.[1] I also enjoy a lovely relationship with my daughters-in-law. I would like to thank them all for showing so much interest in my life history.

Learning to live without David would not have been possible without the constant loving support of my family. Thanks to them, I have continued to live independently, indulge my love of travel, and develop new interests.

In 2010, to celebrate my 80th birthday, I took my sons and daughters-in-law to St Petersburg[2] to show them my childhood home. The building in which we had lived was functioning as an army barracks and everything in the area was extremely rundown. In contrast, the streets near the luxurious Belmond Grand Hotel Europe where we were staying had papier-mâché-like facades hastily erected to impress the international delegates visiting the city. That was not my first return to Russia; my husband and I had been there on a cruise in 2000. On that first trip, troubled

---

1 See family tree on page 222

2 Formerly Leningrad

memories came flooding back and I found it impossible to even cross the threshold of our old apartment.

I am fortunate to still have several maternal cousins living in Moscow. They are the descendants of my great-uncles, Edward, Heinrich and Florian, and it was fascinating to meet up with them after all those years and to reminisce about Musa's converted ballroom apartment on the sixth floor.

My aunt Jenny and uncle Nathan died many years ago, but I have remained in contact with my cousins Mira and Susie in Paris and have met their extended families. I was very upset when my cousin Sonia passed away in Berlin in 2016 – we had a significant shared history and she was one person who truly understood what I had been through as a child. I am pleased to still be in touch with Sonia's husband Moritz and daughter, Anna, who lives in Berlin. I also remain in touch with my first cousin Ilia whose parents were murdered in the Holocaust. After growing up in the children's home in Paris, Ilia was conscripted to fight in the Vietnam War. A year later, he escaped to Cambodia before moving to Thailand. He eventually returned to France where he confronted terrible memories of his traumatic childhood. Ilia ended up making a life for himself in Bangkok.

I remain grateful to have had the opportunity to raise my family in Australia. After surviving a repressive communist regime, I appreciate living in a democratic country that values free speech and freedom of religious expression. Democracy should never be taken for granted and I believe it is worth fighting to protect.

It is my sincere hope that my family continues to grow and prosper in safety and good health.

My cousin Ilia in Bangkok in the 1970s

*(Above) Sonia's husband Moritz, Lily
(an old school friend), Sonia and David
(Below) With Moritz and Sonia, 1988*

My mother-in-law's 90th birthday celebration

David's 70th birthday

(Above) *Avi's* bar mitzvah, *1988*
(Below) *Bradley's* bar mitzvah, *1996*

(Clockwise from above left)
Dean's bar mitzvah, *1999,*
Rodney's bar mitzvah, *1994,*
Ronnie's bar mitzvah, *1990,*
Jonathan's bar mitzvah, *2000*

*(Left) Natalie's bat mitzvah, 1997
(Right) The Ikebana floral display
I created for Natalie (Below) Our home
in Glen Eira Road before we moved to Palm Avenue*

(Above) David's 80th birthday
(Below) Our 50th wedding anniversay

(Above) Ronnie and Amanda's wedding, 2004
(Below) Danny and Libby's wedding, 2005

(Above) Avi and Shahaf's wedding in Israel, 2006
(Below) Jonathan and Kate's wedding, 2013

(Above) Rodney and Lauren's wedding, 2010
(Below) Tobey and Bradley's wedding, 2013

Gabriel and Dean's engagement, 2018
Natalie and Danny's wedding, 2019

With Max and Lizzie's extended family, 2013

With Amanda and Ronnie's four children, 2013

With my gorgeous great-grandchildren, 2017

(Above) Family gathering at Alex and Sue's house, 2018
(Below) With my newest great-grandson Finnegan, 2018

The extended family in 2016 (absent: Finnegan, born August 2018). (Back) Rodney, Flynn, Lauren, Zane, Amanda, Alex, Dean, Taylor, Danny, Natalie, Danny, Ruth, Libby, Kate, Jonathan, Shahaf, Lizzie, Max and Avi (Front) Sue, Rio, Siena, Ofer, Ronnie, Jobie, Ravid, Tobey, Brad and Andie

ACKNOWLEDGEMENTS

I would like to express my deep gratitude to my family for
encouraging me to write the story of my life. In particular,
I would like to thank my grandson Dean Hampel for his repeated
urgings to publish this history for future generations.

This book would not have been possible without co-author
and publisher Romy Moshinsky from Real Film and Publishing.
Over many months I shared the stories of my life with Romy
and she crafted my memories to create this special book. I am
deeply appreciative of her ongoing dedication in bringing my
memoir to life.

I also wish to extend my gratitude to Georgie Raik-Allen, who lent
her valuable insights and discerning editorial eye to this project,
and Abigail Hough for her diligent proofreading.

Finally, thank you to Trisha Garner for her inspired book design.

MY ANCESTORS

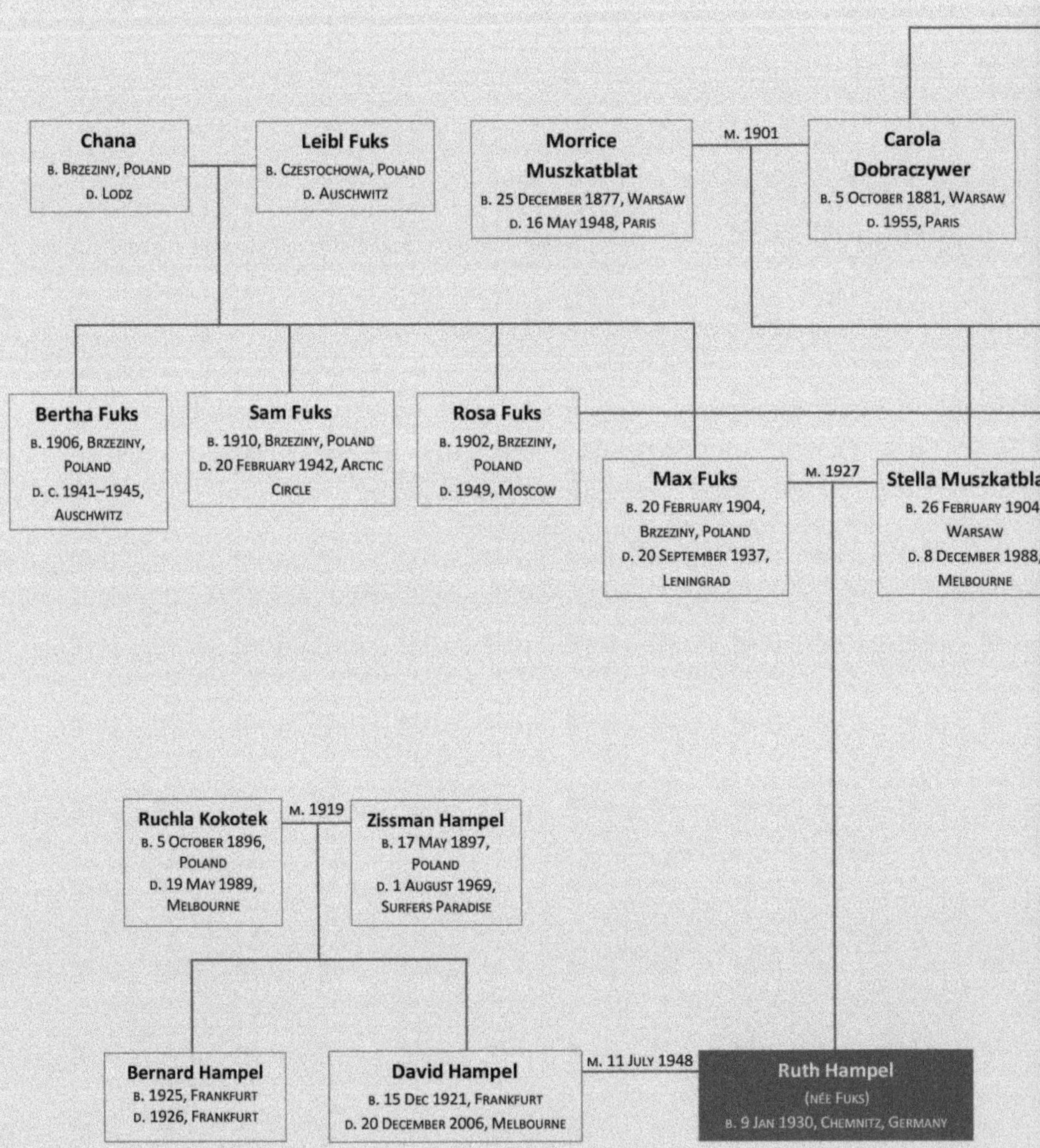

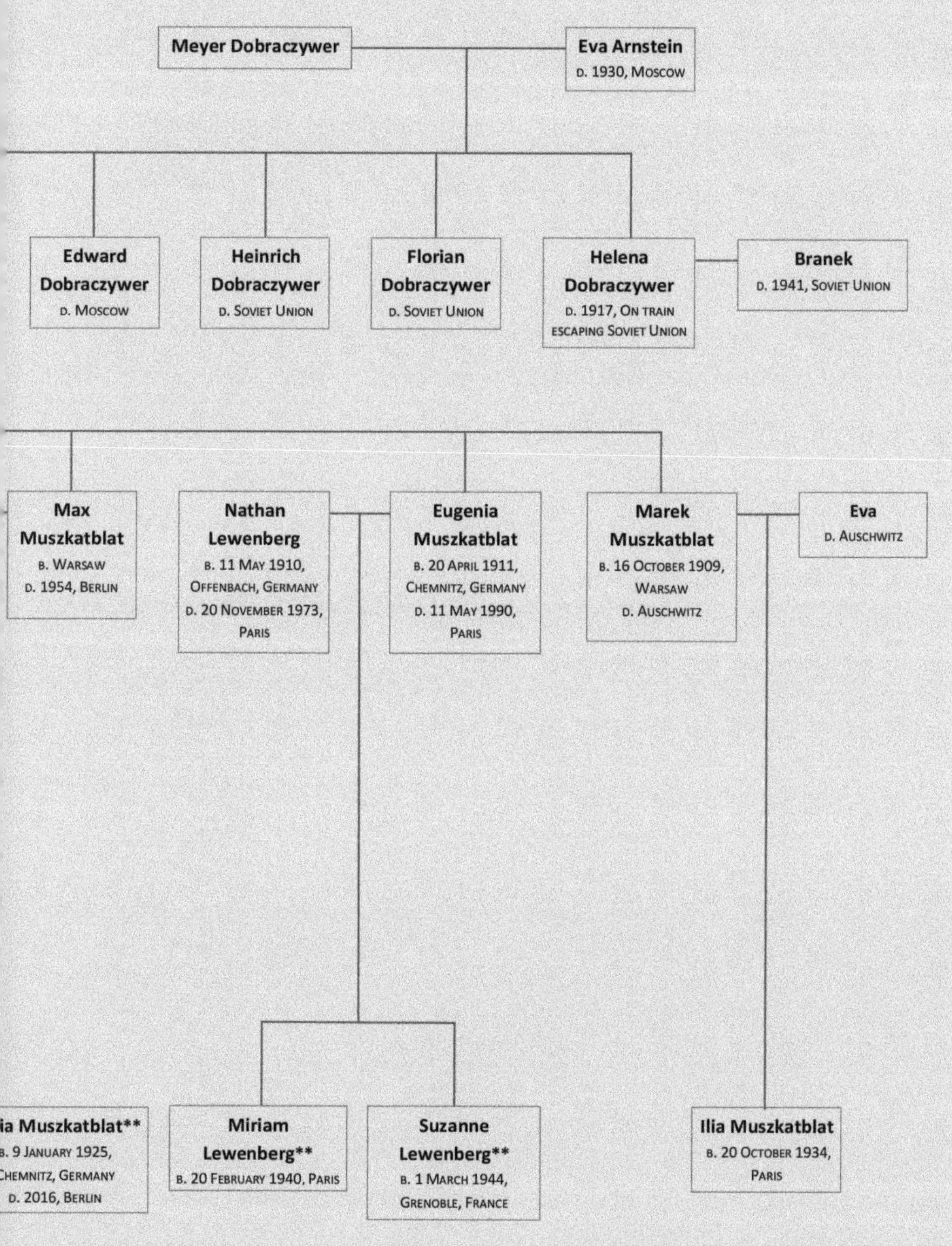

Meyer Dobraczywer
Eva Arnstein
D. 1930, Moscow
Edward Dobraczywer
D. Moscow
Heinrich Dobraczywer
D. Soviet Union
Florian Dobraczywer
D. Soviet Union
Helena Dobraczywer
D. 1917, On train escaping Soviet Union
Branek
D. 1941, Soviet Union
Max Muszkatblat
B. Warsaw
D. 1954, Berlin
Nathan Lewenberg
B. 11 May 1910, Offenbach, Germany
D. 20 November 1973, Paris
Eugenia Muszkatblat
B. 20 April 1911, Chemnitz, Germany
D. 11 May 1990, Paris
Marek Muszkatblat
B. 16 October 1909, Warsaw
D. Auschwitz
Eva
D. Auschwitz
ia Muszkatblat**
B. 9 January 1925, Chemnitz, Germany
D. 2016, Berlin
Miriam Lewenberg**
B. 20 February 1940, Paris
Suzanne Lewenberg**
B. 1 March 1944, Grenoble, France
Ilia Muszkatblat
B. 20 October 1934, Paris
* Stella married again on 31 January 1953 (Maurice Klipper)
** Sonia, Miriam and Suzanne all married. The family bloodline continued into the next generation.

MY DESCENDANTS

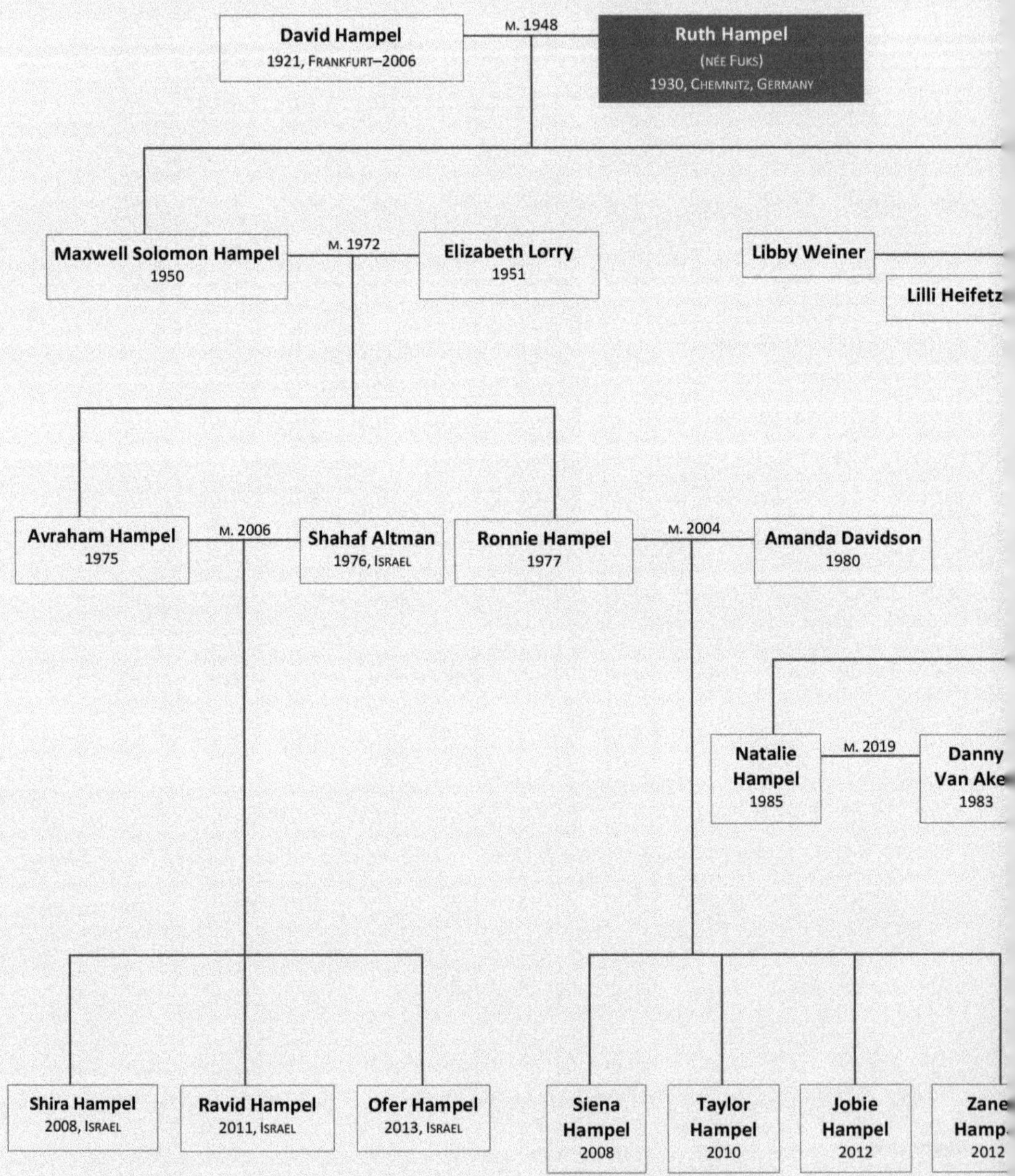

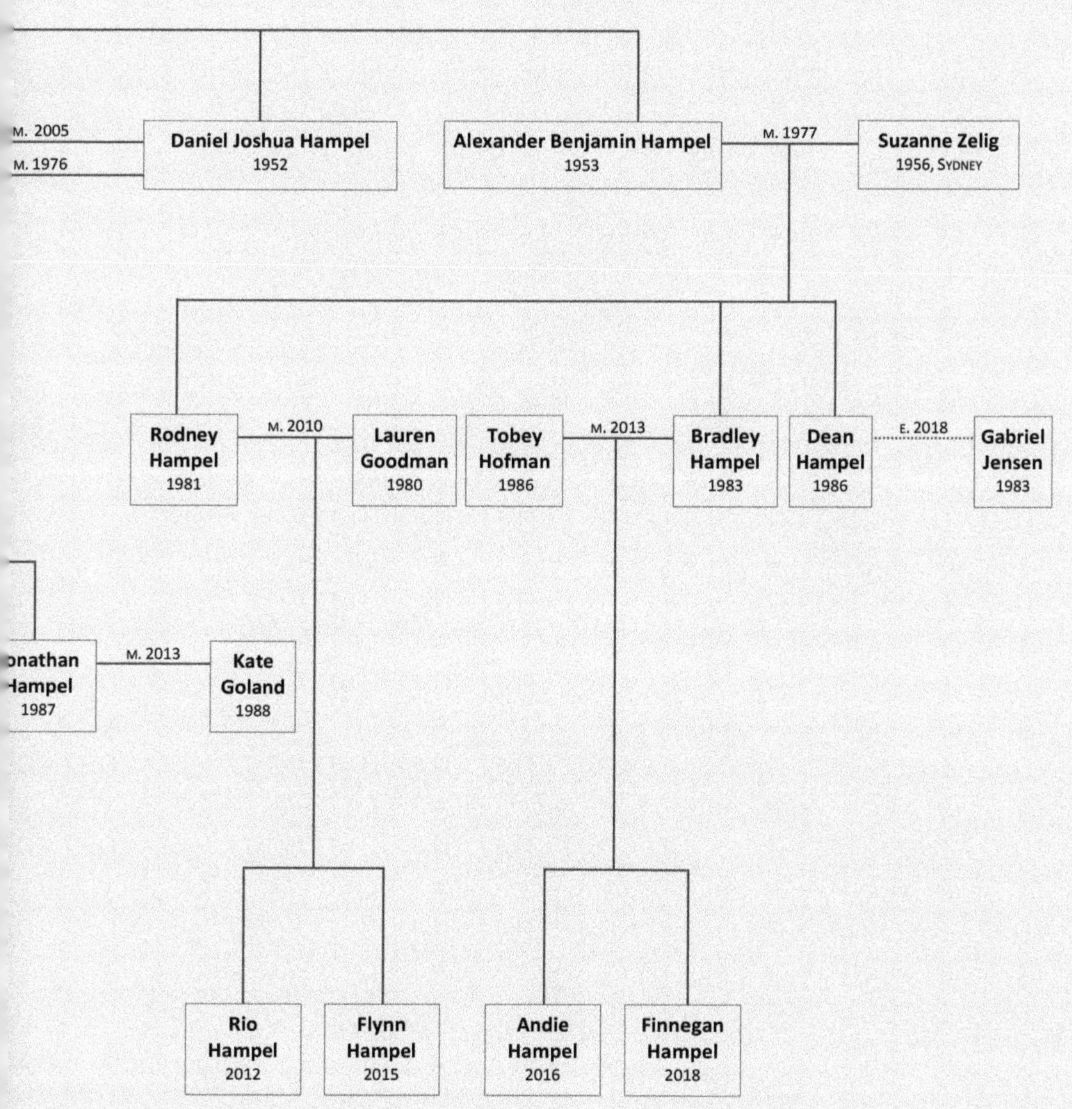

M. 2005
M. 1976
Daniel Joshua Hampel
1952
Alexander Benjamin Hampel
1953
M. 1977
Suzanne Zelig
1956, SYDNEY
Rodney Hampel
1981
M. 2010
Lauren Goodman
1980
Tobey Hofman
1986
M. 2013
Bradley Hampel
1983
Dean Hampel
1986
E. 2018
Gabriel Jensen
1983
Jonathan Hampel
1987
M. 2013
Kate Goland
1988
Rio Hampel
2012
Flynn Hampel
2015
Andie Hampel
2016
Finnegan Hampel
2018

www.ingramcontent.com/pod-product-compliance
Ingram Content Group UK Ltd.
Pitfield, Milton Keynes, MK11 3LW, UK
UKHW061437080726
13597UKWH00033B/16/J